ARIZONA TRIVIA

Compiled by James A. Crutchfield

Rutledge Hill Press®

Nashville, Tennessee

A Division of Thomas Nelson, Inc.

www.ThomasNelson.com

Published by Rutledge Hill Press, a division of Thomas Nelson, Inc., P.O. Box 141000, Nashville, Tennessee 37214.

Library of Congress Cataloging-in-Publication Data

Crutchfield, James Andrew, 1938–
    Arizona trivia / compiled by James A. Crutchfield.
        p. cm.
    ISBN 1-55853-931-X (pbk.)
    1. Arizona —Miscellanea. I. Title.
F811.6 .C78 2001
979.1—dc21

2001004478

Printed in the United States of America

04 05 — 5 4 3 2

ARIZONA TRIVIA

To the fine people of Arizona,
past and present

TABLE OF CONTENTS

PREFACE

Although nearing its one hundredth anniversary, Arizona is still one of the nation's youngest states. Yet it is this very youth—coupled with its citizenry's mixed backgrounds and its great variety of plant and animal life, landforms, terrain, and climates—that makes it a fascinating source of trivia. You will find in the following pages hundreds of questions and answers on all aspects of Arizona's past and present, its people and its economy, its culture and its geography. I hope that you enjoy reading *Arizona Trivia,* the latest in Rutledge Hill Press's continuing series of trivia titles, as much as I enjoyed compiling it.

James A. Crutchfield

GEOGRAPHY

Q. Arizona is bordered by what four states?

A. Utah, New Mexico, California, and Nevada.

—ψ—

Q. What name is given to the place where three states meet Arizona?

A. Four Corners.

—ψ—

Q. Arizona shares a border with what foreign country?

A. Mexico.

—ψ—

Q. How many interstate highways run through Arizona?

A. Six (I-8, I-10, I-40, I-15, I-17, and I-19).

—ψ—

Q. The U.S. Bureau of Land Management owns how many acres in the state?

A. 14.2 million.

—ψ—

Q. The Grand Canyon was formed by what river?

A. The Colorado.

Q. What is the population of Phoenix, Arizona's largest city?

A. 983,403.

—ψ—

Q. What is the largest Native American reservation in the United States?

A. Navajo Indian Reservation, in Arizona.

—ψ—

Q. Where is the highest point in Arizona?

A. Humphrey's Peak (12,643 feet).

—ψ—

Q. Almost the entire western border of Arizona is defined by what river?

A. The Colorado.

—ψ—

Q. Begun as a planned community in the 1950s, what town has such street names as Easy Street, Wampum Way, Ho, and Hum?

A. Carefree.

—ψ—

Q. What is the lowest point in the state?

A. Seventy feet above sea level (on the Colorado River near Yuma).

—ψ—

Q. The geographical center of Arizona is in what county?

A. Yavapai (fifty-five miles southeast of Prescott).

Q. The maximum distance between Arizona's northern and southern borders is how many miles?

A. 395.

Q. When was Tombstone purchased by a group of private individuals and restored to its original appearance?

A. 1957.

Q. What was the original name for Pima County?

A. Ewell County.

Q. What was Maricopa County's population gain between 1990 and 2000?

A. 950,048 (a 44.8% increase).

—ψ—

Q. How does Arizona rank in the nation in land area?

A. Sixth (113,635 square miles).

—ψ—

Q. In what mountains was the legendary Flying Dutchman Mine located?

A. The Superstitions.

—ψ—

Q. In 1848 as a result of the Mexican War, the United States received land that would become what three states and parts of what four others?

A. All of California, Nevada, Utah; parts of Arizona, New Mexico, Colorado, and Wyoming.

Q. What is the county seat of Graham County?

A. Safford.

—ψ—

Q. What five states exceed Arizona in land size?

A. Alaska, Texas, California, Montana, and New Mexico.

—ψ—

Q. According to the 2000 census figures, what is Arizona's population?

A. 5,130,632.

—ψ—

Q. The hottest temperature ever recorded in Arizona reached what mark?

A. 128 degrees, at Lake Havasu City on June 28, 1994.

—ψ—

Q. A winning poker hand provided the name for what town?

A. Show Low (the main street, Deuce of Clubs, memorializes the winning card).

—ψ—

Q. The state contains how many counties?

A. Fifteen.

—ψ—

Q. Derived from a Native American word, *Arizona* means what?

A. "Place of small springs."

Q. The dam that formed Lake Mead was named for what prominent American?

A. President Herbert Hoover.

_ψ_

Q. What is the name for the traditional Navajo home?

A. Hogan.

_ψ_

Q. What Indian reservation is totally contained within the Navajo Indian Reservation?

A. The Hopi Indian Reservation.

_ψ_

Q. The cities of Tempe, Mesa, Glendale, and Sun City are all within the greater metropolitan area of what city?

A. Phoenix.

_ψ_

Q. What two canals bisect Phoenix east to west?

A. The Arizona and Grand.

_ψ_

Q. The Yuma Territorial Prison, used between 1876 and 1909, could house how many inmates at full capacity?

A. Three thousand.

_ψ_

Q. Flowing along the northern city limits of Tucson is what river?

A. The Rillito.

Q. Situated west of Tucson, what large Indian reservation shares a common border with Mexico?

A. Papago.

—ψ—

Q. How does Arizona rank in the nation with respect to amount of federally owned land?

A. Seventh.

—ψ—

Q. The Davis-Monthan Air Force base is situated in what city?

A. Tucson.

—ψ—

Q. At what national monument may one visit a ranch house and two bunkhouses preserved as a tribute to pioneers who explored, settled, and developed the Southwest?

A. Pipe Spring.

—ψ—

Q. Between what two cities is the Barry M. Goldwater Air Force Range located?

A. Yuma and Casa Grande (south of I-8).

—ψ—

Q. What Mexican town is just across the international border from Nogales, Arizona?

A. Nogales.

—ψ—

Q. For whom was the Sitgreaves National Forest named?

A. Capt. Lorenzo Sitgreaves, a U.S. Army engineer.

Q. Flagstaff is situated at the junction of what two interstate highways?

A. I-40 and I-17.

Q. What is the average elevation of Arizona?

A. 4,100 feet.

Q. In the extreme southeastern corner of the state lies what county?

A. Cochise.

Q. When was La Paz, the state's newest county, formed?

A. January 1, 1983.

Q. Referring to the Grand Canyon, what U.S. president said, "You cannot improve on it. The ages have been at work on it, and man can only mar it."

A. Theodore Roosevelt in 1903.

Q. By what name is the Papago Indian tribe now known?

A. Tohono O'odham.

Q. In what city is Arizona State University located?

A. Tempe.

Q. What area of badlands displaying a variety of hues lies partially in the Petrified Forest National Park?

A. The Painted Desert.

—ψ—

Q. What Wyoming engineer first proposed damming the Colorado River?

A. Dr. Elwood Mead, who is commemorated by Lake Mead.

—ψ—

Q. Why are tours not allowed in the Montezuma Castle National Monument?

A. As a preservative measure, but a self-guiding trail offers good views of the five-story castle.

—ψ—

Q. Between 1990 and 2000 by what percentage did Arizona's population grow?

A. 40 percent.

—ψ—

Q. According to legend, what happened at Apache Leap Cliff, near the silver-mining town of Superior?

A. Rather than be captured by the U.S. cavalry, seventy-five warriors leaped to their deaths.

—ψ—

Q. In 1970 what metropolis did Phoenix pass as the most populous city in the Rocky Mountain region?

A. Denver.

—ψ—

Q. Lake Mead contains how many miles of shoreline?

A. 550 (compared to its straight-line length of 115 miles).

Q. What county has the largest population in Arizona?

A. Maricopa (3,072,149).

—ψ—

Q. With a population of 8,008, what county has the fewest people?

A. Greenlee.

—ψ—

Q. For whom was Greenlee County named?

A. Marc Greenlee, a prospector.

—ψ—

Q. For how long has the volcano in Sunset Crater National Monument been dormant?

A. Nearly one thousand years.

—ψ—

Q. How much territory does the Grand Canyon include?

A. About 277 square miles.

—ψ—

Q. Such large companies as IBM, Garrett AiResearch, and Hughes Aircraft have operations in what city?

A. Tucson.

—ψ—

Q. When was Parker Dam completed on the Colorado River?

A. 1934.

Q. Arizona has what two main land regions?

A. Colorado Plateau, and Basin and Range.

—ψ—

Q. The North Rim of the Grand Canyon is how many feet higher than the South Rim?

A. One thousand.

—ψ—

Q. Mesilla served as the capital of what political entity?

A. Confederate Territory of Arizona.

—ψ—

Q. Upon the banks of what river does Tucson lie?

A. The Santa Cruz.

—ψ—

Q. Through which major Arizona city did the legendary Route 66 pass?

A. Flagstaff.

—ψ—

Q. For what purpose was Bullhead City built in 1945?

A. To provide homes for workers constructing Davis Dam.

—ψ—

Q. What three states meet near Yuma?

A. Arizona and California in the U.S. and Baja California in Mexico.

Q. What was another name suggested for Arizona in preterritorial days?

A. Gadsonia, derived from the Gadsden Purchase.

—ψ—

Q. Compared to other state capitals, how does Phoenix rank in size?

A. First.

—ψ—

Q. How many miles of inland water does Arizona contain?

A. 492.

—ψ—

Q. The famous London Bridge was moved to what location?

A. Lake Havasu City.

—ψ—

Q. How does Arizona rank in the nation with respect to non-English-speaking population?

A. Sixth.

—ψ—

Q. Containing fewer than 1,300 square miles, what is the smallest county in Arizona?

A. Santa Cruz.

—ψ—

Q. What county, comprising nearly 19,000 square miles, has the largest area?

A. Coconino.

Q. The state maintains how many Indian reservations?

A. Six.

—ψ—

Q. After its heyday in gold-mining times, what town eleven miles northeast of Wickenburg officially became a ghost town when its post office was discontinued in 1939?

A. Constellation.

—ψ—

Q. How high are the rock walls within Canyon de Chelly?

A. One thousand to twelve hundred feet.

—ψ—

Q. Monument Valley consists of how many acres?

A. About 30,000.

—ψ—

Q. What is Arizona's fourth largest city?

A. Glendale (population around 211,000).

—ψ—

Q. In 1882 Glendale was founded because of what industry?

A. Cotton farming.

—ψ—

Q. For whom was the town of Douglas named when it was founded in 1901?

A. James Douglas.

Q. What state lies directly east of Arizona?

A. New Mexico.

—ψ—

Q. What state lies directly north of Arizona?

A. Utah.

—ψ—

Q. What two states lie directly west of Arizona?

A. California and Nevada.

—ψ—

Q. How many businesses highlighted in the 2000 Fortune 500 survey of the 100 Best Places in the U.S. to Work are located in the greater Phoenix area?

A. Thirty-eight.

—ψ—

Q. What was the smallest city counted in the 2000 census?

A. Mohave Ranch Estates, south of Bullhead City, with a population of twenty-eight.

—ψ—

Q. In what county are the Vulture Mountains?

A. Maricopa County.

—ψ—

Q. Where is Paramore Crater located?

A. In the extreme southeast part of the state in Cochise County.

Q. What dam's impounded waters irrigate the Salt River valley?

A. Roosevelt Dam.

—ψ—

Q. What was Yuma County's original name?

A. Castle Dome County.

—ψ—

Q. What is the altitude of Apache Pass?

A. 5,115 feet.

—ψ—

Q. Where can one visit Biosphere 2 Center?

A. Between Catalina and Oracle.

—ψ—

Q. Where in Arizona were almost eighteen thousand Japanese-Americans interned in 1942?

A. Poston.

—ψ—

Q. In 1903 a New York newspaper reporter called what mining village "the wickedest town in America"?

A. Jerome.

—ψ—

Q. What is the average depth of the Grand Canyon?

A. About one mile.

Q. What was the median price for existing single-family homes during the first quarter of 2000 in Phoenix compared to Tucson?

A. $130,900 for Phoenix, $114,100 for Tucson.

—ψ—

Q. What two rivers join to form the Salt River?

A. The Black and the White.

—ψ—

Q. What town was founded in 1957 to accommodate construction workers on Glen Canyon Dam?

A. Page.

—ψ—

Q. A 560-foot-tall white jet of water that shoots above the town for fifteen minutes every hour on the hour entertains visitors to what community?

A. Fountain Hills.

—ψ—

Q. What dam is located on the Bill Williams River?

A. Alamo.

—ψ—

Q. What was the occupation of Bill Williams for whom the river was named?

A. Fur trapper and mountain man.

—ψ—

Q. Where can one find the Grand Canyon Caverns?

A. Just south of Arizona Highway 66 near the town of Nelson.

Q. What is the official name of the Phoenix airport?

A. Sky Harbor International Airport.

—ψ—

Q. How did Flagstaff get its name?

A. A lone pine tree discovered in a nearby valley was stripped of its branches and used as a flagstaff for the Fourth of July celebration in 1876.

—ψ—

Q. What is the elevation of Zihi-Dush-Jhini Peak on the Hopi Indian Reservation?

A. 7,107 feet.

—ψ—

Q. What boatman and artist accompanying the Powell exploratory expedition in the nineteenth century had a mountain named for him?

A. Frederich S. Dellenbaugh (Mount Dellenbaugh).

—ψ—

Q. Where is Colorado City located?

A. In extreme northern Arizona, just south of the Utah border.

—ψ—

Q. In 1872 what present-day city was named Hayden's Ferry for Charles Turnbull Hayden, who operated a ferry there across the Salt River?

A. Tempe.

—ψ—

Q. Upon what river is Coolidge Dam located?

A. The Gila.

Q. What was the original name of the Robinson-May department stores?

A. M. Goldwater and Brother.

—ψ—

Q. Jerusalem Mountain is in what group of mountains?

A. The Mescal Mountains.

—ψ—

Q. What was the original name for Hoover Dam?

A. Boulder.

—ψ—

Q. Which one of the six Apache tribes has become extinct?

A. Lipan.

—ψ—

Q. For whom is Prescott National Forest named?

A. The historian William H. Prescott.

—ψ—

Q. According to the 2000 census, Arizona has how many households?

A. 1,901,327.

—ψ—

Q. At the mouth of Canyon Bonito, one can visit what first U.S. military post established in Arizona in 1851?

A. Fort Defiance.

Q. Native Americans make up what percentage of the state's population?

A. 5 percent.

Q. White Arizonans account for what percentage of state residents?

A. 75.5 percent.

Q. What was the last county to be organized in the nineteenth century?

A. Santa Cruz County, established on March 15, 1899.

Q. One of the largest and most popular retirement communities in the nation, what city of over forty thousand people is in the Phoenix metropolitan area?

A. Sun City/Sun City West.

Q. What is the largest single employer in southern Arizona?

A. Fort Huachuca, of the U.S. Army.

Q. Where may one visit a POW camp exhibit portraying life at the largest POW camp in Arizona, housing more than fifty-six hundred prisoners of war?

A. McFarland State Historic Park, in Florence.

Q. What was the original name for the town of Sierra Vista?

A. Frye.

Q. For what is the town of Cottonwood best known today?

A. It is a popular retirement village.

—ψ—

Q. Between 1998 and 1999, what were the only counties to lose population?

A. Apache and Greenlee.

—ψ—

Q. La Paz County gained how many people between 1998 and 1999?

A. Thirty-seven.

—ψ—

Q. Why was Hayden's Ferry renamed Tempe in 1878?

A. Because the residents thought it resembled the Vale of Tempe in ancient Greece.

—ψ—

Q. Bordering the Grand Canyon on the south are what two Indian reservations?

A. Havasupai and Hualapai.

—ψ—

Q. How many of Arizona's counties are named after Indian tribes?

A. Seven.

—ψ—

Q. The town of Nogales was established for what purpose?

A. As a customs checkpoint to control cattle movement between the United States and Mexico.

Q. What museum does Bullhead City feature?

A. Colorado River Historical Society & Museum.

—ψ—

Q. What is Pinal County's nickname?

A. "The County in the Shadow of the Superstitions."

—ψ—

Q. What was the coldest temperature ever recorded in Arizona?

A. 40 degrees below zero (at Hawley Lake, January 7, 1971).

—ψ—

Q. In what town is the John Wesley Powell Memorial Museum?

A. Page.

—ψ—

Q. Within the Hopi Indian Reservation are what two pueblos, both among the oldest in America?

A. Walpi and Oraibi.

—ψ—

Q. In the Apache language, what is the meaning of the word *Tuzigoot,* as in Tuzigoot National Monument?

A. "Crooked water."

—ψ—

Q. How long has the Oraibi pueblo been continuously occupied?

A. Since around A.D. 1100.

Q. What unique distinction does Oraibi have?

A. It is believed to be the longest continuously occupied community in America.

—ψ—

Q. When was national monument status conferred on Tuzigoot?

A. 1939.

—ψ—

Q. When was the territorial capital moved to Phoenix?

A. 1889.

—ψ—

Q. Approximately how long ago were the trees in the Petrified Forest National Park growing?

A. 180 million years.

—ψ—

Q. What Indian culture was responsible for the present-day ruins in Tonto National Monument?

A. The Salado people.

—ψ—

Q. What does the word *salado* mean in Spanish?

A. "Salty."

—ψ—

Q. When did the Salado people arrive in the vicinity of today's Tonto National Monument?

A. Around A.D. 900.

Q. The Navajo National Monument contains the ruins of what three awe-inspiring cliff dwellings?

A. Betatakin, Keet Seel, and Inscription House.

—ψ—

Q. Keet Seel, the largest and best-preserved cliff dwelling in Arizona, dates from what years?

A. Approximately A.D. 1250 to 1300.

—ψ—

Q. Who discovered Betatakin in 1909?

A. Byron Cummings and John Wetherill.

—ψ—

Q. In the Navajo language what is the meaning of *keet seel*?

A. "Broken pottery."

—ψ—

Q. The Casa Grande Ruins National Monument is within the city limits of what present-day town?

A. Coolidge.

—ψ—

Q. What three missions founded by Father Eusebio Francisco Kino are still to be seen along Interstate 19, south of Tucson?

A. San Xavier del Bac, Tumacacori, and Guevavi.

—ψ—

Q. How many named mesas does the Hopi Indian Reservation contain?

A. Three, called First, Second, and Third Mesas.

Q. Where is the Navajo Tribal Museum?

A. Window Rock.

—ψ—

Q. Maricopa County has been given what nickname?

A. "Arizona's Valley of the Sun."

—ψ—

Q. What is considered to be the oldest continuously inhabited city in America?

A. Tucson (based on the fact that people of the Hohokam culture lived on the site as early as A.D. 100).

—ψ—

Q. Coconino County's name comes from a Havasupai word meaning what?

A. "Little water."

—ψ—

Q. What county gets its name from a Native American word meaning "deer"?

A. Pinal.

—ψ—

Q. What is Pinal County's seat of government?

A. Florence.

—ψ—

Q. What is the approximate population of the Navajo Indian Reservation?

A. About 175,000.

Q. What is the maximum distance between Arizona's eastern and western borders?

A. 340 miles.

—ψ—

Q. Where is Northern Arizona University located?

A. Flagstaff.

—ψ—

Q. What is the state's highest mountain group?

A. The San Francisco Peaks.

—ψ—

Q. What is Arizona's second largest city?

A. Tucson.

—ψ—

Q. What is America's largest ghost town?

A. Jerome.

—ψ—

Q. Each year Phoenix receives an average of how many days of precipitation?

A. Thirty-five.

—ψ—

Q. How many more days of precipitation, on the average, does Flagstaff receive than Phoenix annually?

A. Forty (seventy-five compared to thirty-five).

Q. Where in Arizona is daylight savings time observed?

A. Only on the Navajo Indian Reservation.

—ψ—

Q. How long is the Colorado River?

A. 1450 miles.

—ψ—

Q. What is the origin of the name Tucson?

A. The Native American term *chukshon*, meaning "spring at the foot of the black hill," referring to the springs once found along the banks of the nearby river.

—ψ—

Q. What is the maximum speed limit on Arizona interstate highways?

A. Seventy-five miles per hour.

—ψ—

Q. Where is the administrative headquarters for the Navajo Indian Reservation located?

A. Tuba City.

—ψ—

Q. Where is White Mesa Natural Bridge?

A. On the Navajo Indian Reservation south of Kaibito.

—ψ—

Q. What highway crosses Hoover Dam?

A. U.S. Highway 93.

Q. Lengthwise, how does the Colorado River rank among U.S. rivers?

A. Fifth.

—ψ—

Q. Where is the Apache leader Cochise buried?

A. He was interred in secret in the Dragoon Mountains in an area now called Cochise's Stronghold, but the actual gravesite is unknown.

—ψ—

Q. What does *colorado* mean in Spanish?

A. Red..

—ψ—

Q. What two U.S. cities tie for the dubious honor of having the highest average July temperature?

A. Phoenix and Las Vegas, Nevada (105 degrees Fahrenheit).

—ψ—

Q. Besides the Sonoran Desert, what other desert occupies much of Arizona's area?

A. The Mohave Desert.

—ψ—

Q. How does the entire Sonoran Desert compare in size to other world deserts?

A. It is the eighth largest.

—ψ—

Q. Why was the town of Payson named for someone who was never there?

A. It was named for a senator who secured the U. S. Post Office for the village.

Q. Who named the Colorado River?

A. The Spanish explorer and priest, Francisco Garcés.

—ψ—

Q. Covering much of southern Arizona, the U.S. part of the Sonoran Desert covers how many square miles?

A. Seventy thousand

—ψ—

Q. What is the name of the cemetery at Tombstone?

A. Boot Hill.

—ψ—

Q. The Colorado River drains parts of how many states?

A. Seven (plus Mexico).

—ψ—

Q. What is the largest tributary of the Colorado River?

A. The Little Colorado River.

—ψ—

Q. Where are the two sources of the Colorado River?

A. One of its forks (the Colorado River) begins in Grand Lake in Colorado and the other (the Green River) begins in south-western Wyoming.

—ψ—

Q. In the early 1900s where was the entire flow of the Colorado River diverted?

A. To create the Salton Sea in California.

Q. What is Greenlee County's nickname?

A. "The Place Where Coronado Walked."

—ψ—

Q. The Grand Canyon has how many visitors each year?

A. More than 5 million.

—ψ—

Q. Morris Udall, John F. Kennedy, and Christopher Columbus are all remembered in Tucson by what?

A. Parks named after them.

—ψ—

Q. What thoroughfare grew up along the pathway used by Lt. Col. Philip St. George Cooke when he led 450 Mormon volunteers from Santa Fe to San Diego?

A. The Gila Trail.

—ψ—

Q. After whom is the town of Wickenburg named?

A. Henry Wickenburg, who discovered the nearby Vulture Gold Mine.

—ψ—

Q. How did Henry Wickenburg discover gold that would yield more than $20 million in the years after 1863?

A. In a rock he was throwing after his escaping mule.

—ψ—

Q. In whose honor was Luke Air Force Base named?

A. Arizonan Frank Luke, a World War I ace pilot and Medal of Honor winner.

Q. When is Arizona's monsoon season?

A. July, August, and September.

Q. Which Indian tribe dwells upon the Fort McDowell Indian Reservation?

A. The Yavapai.

Q. The discovery of the Copper Queen Lode in the 1880s made what town become the largest cosmopolitan center between St. Louis and San Francisco?

A. Bisbee.

Q. Opened on November 12, 1999, what is Arizona's newest state park?

A. Kartchner Caverns, near Benson.

Q. When were the Kartchner Caverns discovered?

A. 1974, but they were not announced publicly until 1988.

Q. What was Benson's original claim to fame?

A. It was a railroad town on the Southern Pacific railway line.

Q. Indian reservations occupy what percentage of Arizona's total land area?

A. 27 percent.

Q. What town is Apache County's seat of government?

A. Saint Johns.

—ψ—

Q. Casa Grande, meaning "big house" in Spanish, received its name from what source?

A. The nearby four-story structure built by the Hohokam Indians around A.D. 1350.

—ψ—

Q. What town is the main stop on the longest existing stretch of historic Route 66?

A. Kingman.

—ψ—

Q. Between what towns can travelers traverse 140 miles of historic Route 66?

A. Ashfork and Topock.

—ψ—

Q. How did Globe receive its name?

A. From a globe-shaped piece of pure silver reputedly found nearby.

—ψ—

Q. Where are the Chocolate Mountains located?

A. Between I-8 and I-10 near the California border.

—ψ—

Q. According to the 2000 census, what percentage of the Arizona population is black?

A. 3.1 percent.

Q. Bartlett and Horsehoe Dams are located on what river?

A. The Verde.

Q. The Aravaipa and the San Pedro Rivers are tributaries to what river?

A. The Gila.

Q. What two Arizona counties were organized in the twentieth century?

A. Greenlee and La Paz.

Q. The territorial capital was located in what two other places before it was moved to Phoenix?

A. Prescott and Tucson.

Q. How did the town of Prescott get started?

A. It grew up around the log house built for the first territorial governor to live in after he established his headquarters at nearby Fort Whipple.

Q. What three counties were all organized on December 21, 1864?

A. Yuma, Yavapai, and Mohave.

Q. What Mexican town lies just across the international border from Douglas?

A. Agua Prieta.

Q. In what county can the towns of Gu Vo, Why, Ko Vaya, and Pan Tak be found?

A. Pima.

—ψ—

Q. What pass in the Dos Cabezas Mountains was made famous by the Bascom Affair in 1861?

A. Apache.

—ψ—

Q. What is a dragoon, as in the Dragoon Mountains?

A. A mounted soldier or a cavalryman.

—ψ—

Q. According to the 2000 census, what percentage of Arizonans own their homes?

A. 68 percent.

—ψ—

Q. Besides surveying the wagon road from Fort Defiance to the Colorado River, Edward F. Beale was the leader of what unusual 1840s experiment by the U.S. Army?

A. Using camels in the desert.

—ψ—

Q. Santa Cruz County gets its name from what Spanish expression?

A. "Holy cross."

—ψ—

Q. Other than Arizona, what states have a Graham County?

A. Kansas and North Carolina.

ENTERTAINMENT

Q. The original *Tonight Show* was hosted by what late Phoenix resident?

A. Steve Allen.

Q. What famous clown lived in Tombstone?

A. Emmett Kelly.

Q. Cowboy singer Tex Ritter married what aspiring actress from Prescott?

A. Dorothy Fay Southworth.

Q. Tom Mix died in an auto accident near what Arizona town?

A. Florence.

Q. Hollywood actress Anne Baxter was the granddaughter of what famous architect with Arizona connections?

A. Frank Lloyd Wright.

Q. Where is the Rex Allen Arizona Cowboy Museum to be found?

A. Willcox.

—ψ—

Q. What 1960s TV series did Ronald Reagan host from Apache Junction?

A. *Death Valley Days.*

—ψ—

Q. Country music legend Glen Campbell calls what city home?

A. Phoenix.

—ψ—

Q. The song "Only a Bird in a Gilded Cage" was inspired by what opera house saloon?

A. The Bird Cage in Tombstone.

—ψ—

Q. What noted film director moved to Scottsdale as a young boy?

A. Steven Spielberg.

—ψ—

Q. What was country music singer Marty Robbins's hometown?

A. Glendale.

—ψ—

Q. What unique name was given to Marty Robbins's wife?

A. Marizona, derived from the fact that she was born in Maricopa County, Arizona.

Q. When was the first Hollywood film made in Arizona?

A. 1923.

Q. What were the first two feature movies filmed in Arizona?

A. *To the Last Man* and *The Call of the Canyon.*

Q. What noted Phoenix country singer starred with John Wayne in the movie *True Grit*?

A. Glen Campbell.

Q. What was Hollywood heartthrob Rudolph Valentino's first Arizona film?

A. *Son of the Sheik.*

Q. Filmed in 1936 near Yuma, what movie starred Hollywood legends Marlene Dietrich, Charles Boyer, and Basil Rathbone?

A. *The Garden of Allah.*

Q. What was director John Ford's favorite Arizona filming location?

A. Monument Valley.

Q. Scenes from *Gunfight at the O. K. Corral* were filmed at what Arizona location?

A. Old Tucson.

Q. Who is known as the "godfather of Phoenix-area guitarists"?

A. Al Casey.

—ψ—

Q. What Jerry Lewis movie was filmed on location in Yuma?

A. *Sad Sack.*

—ψ—

Q. Shot in Sedona, what 1939 movie featured Errol Flynn, Olivia de Havilland, and Ann Sheridan?

A. *Dodge City.*

—ψ—

Q. What is Arizona's leading industry?

A. Tourism.

—ψ—

Q. Who was the producer and director of the movie *Northwest Mounted Police* shot in 1940 in Flagstaff?

A. Cecil B. DeMille.

—ψ—

Q. In 1971 what country music legends broadcast their own TV show from Carefree?

A. Johnny Cash and June Carter Cash.

—ψ—

Q. Clint Eastwood directed and starred in what western filmed in Patagonia and Mescal?

A. *The Outlaw Josey Wales.*

Q. Who co-starred with Clint Eastwood in *The Outlaw Josey Wales*?

A. Chief Dan George.

—ψ—

Q. In what city's Little America Hotel are more than two million Christmas lights displayed during the holiday season?

A. Flagstaff.

—ψ—

Q. Michael Douglas starred in what movie that was filmed in Nogales?

A. *Traffic*.

—ψ—

Q. The Phoenix area is home to what longtime host of ABC's *20/20*?

A. Hugh Downs.

—ψ—

Q. The town of Patagonia was the location for what Hollywood musical?

A. *Oklahoma*.

—ψ—

Q. When was the movie set Old Tucson built?

A. 1939.

—ψ—

Q. For what movie was Old Tucson specifically built?

A. *Arizona*.

Q. When was Old Tucson destroyed by fire?

A. 1955.

Q. Born in Flagstaff, cowboy sidekick Andy Devine was raised in what town?

A. Kingman.

Q. What was the first Hollywood feature filmed in Monument Valley?

A. *Stagecoach.*

Q. Who were the three stars in *Stagecoach*?

A. John Wayne, Andy Devine, and Claire Trevor.

Q. What 1939 Cary Grant movie was shot in Yuma?

A. *Gunga Din.*

Q. From what city does award-winning singer Linda Ronstadt hail?

A. Tucson.

Q. In 1911, when Cecil B. DeMille left New York looking for a suitable location for the burgeoning movie business, what Arizona town did he consider?

A. Flagstaff.

Q. What do Lynda Carter, Nick Nolte, Jack Elam, and Wayne Newton have in common?

A. Being raised in the Phoenix region.

—ψ—

Q. Where is the Tom Mix Memorial?

A. Florence.

—ψ—

Q. During the 1920s what was Tom Mix's weekly salary?

A. Seventeen thousand dollars.

—ψ—

Q. Who was the only Hollywood cowboy who ever really worked as a cowboy?

A. Rex Allen Sr., a native of Willcox.

—ψ—

Q. What was the name of Rex Allen's horse?

A. Koko.

—ψ—

Q. What traveling actress became Wyatt Earp's mistress?

A. Josephine Sarah Marcus.

—ψ—

Q. Director John Ford filmed what three cavalry movies in Monument Valley starring John Wayne?

A. *Fort Apache*, *She Wore a Yellow Ribbon*, and *Rio Grande*.

Q. What Arizona native starred with John Wayne in *She Wore a Yellow Ribbon* and *Rio Grande*?

A. Ben Johnson.

—ψ—

Q. Clark Gable and Carole Lombard honeymooned March 18, 1939, at what hotel, where their suite is now a major attraction?

A. Oatman Hotel, in Oatman, an authentic preserved mining town.

—ψ—

Q. What musical event is scheduled each September in Sedona?

A. Jazz on the Rocks.

—ψ—

Q. The Barleen Family Country Music Dinner show at Apache Junction, seating five hundred people, has changed its name to what?

A. Arizona Opry.

—ψ—

Q. Phoenix has what two Spanish-language radio stations?

A. KNAI, 88.3, and KVVA, 107.1.

—ψ—

Q. For the 1932 twelve-episode serial *The Three Musketeers*, starring a young John Wayne, what historical building was used as a French Foreign Legion fort?

A. The Territorial Prison at Yuma.

—ψ—

Q. The Chocolate Affaire, an event heralded as a festival of chocolate and romance, takes place each February in what city?

A. Glendale.

Q. In the 1950 movie *Broken Arrow*, Jeff Chandler portrayed what Native American chief?

A. Cochise.

—ψ—

Q. In what city did Bob Nolan, the legendary leader of the Sons of the Pioneers, attend high school?

A. Tucson.

—ψ—

Q. What 1991 action movie filmed at Tucson and Mesa starred Nicholas Cage and Tommy Lee Jones?

A. *Firebirds*.

—ψ—

Q. Episodes of the TV show *Rawhide* were shot at what Arizona location?

A. Nogales.

—ψ—

Q. Where was the classic western movie *3:10 to Yuma* shot?

A. Willcox.

—ψ—

Q. What actors starred in *3:10 to Yuma*?

A. Glenn Ford and Van Heflin.

—ψ—

Q. When was Tempe's first movie theater opened?

A. 1933.

Q. A one-time Phoenix resident, what cartoonist created *The Family Circus*?

A. Bill Keane.

—ψ—

Q. Which Fleetwood Mac singer grew up in Phoenix?

A. Stevie Nicks.

—ψ—

Q. Actor Nick Nolte attended what Arizona college?

A. Phoenix College.

—ψ—

Q. What was the only film acting legend Spencer Tracy made in Arizona?

A. *Broken Lance.*

—ψ—

Q. In the movie *The Greatest Story Ever Told*, what Arizona body of water was used to depict the Sea of Galilee?

A. Lake Powell.

—ψ—

Q. What Miss Arizona became Miss America in 1949?

A. Jacque Mercer, from Litchfield.

—ψ—

Q. In 1965 who moved up from Miss Arizona to Miss America?

A. Vonda Kay Van Dyke, from Phoenix.

Q. What rock star attended Cortez High School in Phoenix?

A. Alice Cooper.

—ψ—

Q. What is Alice Cooper's real name?

A. Vincent Damon Furnier.

—ψ—

Q. Tanya Tucker, Linda Ronstadt, Lynda Carter, and Duane Eddy have all appeared with what Phoenix TV host?

A. Lew King.

—ψ—

Q. What TV series did Lynda Carter star in?

A. *Wonder Woman.*

—ψ—

Q. What Arizona guitar player was a 1994 Rock and Roll Hall of Fame inductee?

A. Duane Eddy.

—ψ—

Q. What Hollywood husband-wife team once had a home in Kino Springs?

A. Stewart Granger and Jean Simmons.

—ψ—

Q. "Baby I'm Yours" and "He's So Fine "were recorded by what Phoenix singing star?

A. Jody Miller.

Q. John Wayne once owned what Arizona ranch?

A. 26 Bar Ranch.

—ψ—

Q. The 1939 movie *Arizona* had what two stars?

A. William Holden and Jean Arthur.

—ψ—

Q. Who made famous the song, "By the Time I Get to Phoenix"?

A. Glen Campbell.

—ψ—

Q. Where is former Glendale resident Marty Robbins buried?

A. Nashville.

—ψ—

Q. The award-winning movie *The Shootist*, starring John Wayne, was based on the book with the same name by what Scottsdale writer?

A. Glendon Swarthout.

—ψ—

Q. With what singing trio did official Arizona state historian Marshall Trimble begin his musical career?

A. The Gin Mill Three.

—ψ—

Q. What dude ranch in Wickenburg was operated by cowboy entertainer Romaine Lowdermilk?

A. The Kay El Bar Ranch.

Q. Who was the first black Miss Arizona?

A. Cara Jackson, in 1995.

—ψ—

Q. Some scenes in *Raiders of the Lost Ark* were filmed in what Arizona town?

A. Yuma.

—ψ—

Q. The town of Kingman bestowed what honor upon Andy Devine?

A. Naming a street named after him.

—ψ—

Q. What native Arizonan, a singer, poet, and writer, is also state historian?

A. Marshall Trimble.

—ψ—

Q. In what year did the song "Ragtime Cowboy Joe," which depicts an Arizona cowboy, appear?

A. 1912.

—ψ—

Q. What Arizona location was used in filming the movie *A Man Called Horse*?

A. Flagstaff.

—ψ—

Q. Starring William Boyd and Gabby Hayes, the 1937 movie *The Texas Trail* was filmed in what Arizona location?

A. Sedona.

Q. The Paseo de Casas tours, held annually in May in Jerome, features the homes of workers and officials in what industry?

A. Mining.

Q. Where was *My Darling Clementine,* starring Henry Fonda, Victor Mature, and Linda Darnell, shot?

A. Monument Valley.

Q. The 1986 American Music Awards were televised from what location?

A. Old Tucson.

Q. In 2001 a small Scottsdale company purchased what noted American arms manufacturer?

A. Smith & Wesson, makers of fine handguns.

Q. Radio commentator Paul Harvey calls what city home?

A. Phoenix.

Q. At what establishment in Tombstone did Enrico Caruso and Sarah Bernhardt once perform?

A. The Bird Cage Theater.

Q. When he filmed in Monument Valley, where did director John Ford make his headquarters?

A. Gouldings Trading Post.

Q. What native of Globe and graduate of Phoenix Union High School has played the bad guy in scores of western movies?

A. Jack Elam.

—ψ—

Q. What aspiring young actor co-starred with John Wayne in *Red River*?

A. Montgomery Clift.

—ψ—

Q. What Arizona actor played in scores of westerns, including *Tom Horn*, *The Grey Fox*, and *Comes a Horseman*?

A. Richard Farnsworth.

—ψ—

Q. Marilyn Monroe made what movie in Arizona?

A. *Bus Stop.*

—ψ—

Q. The Annual Arizona Old-Time Fiddlers Jam and Country Store Bazaar and Car Show takes place each January in what city?

A. Casa Grande.

—ψ—

Q. In 1950 Ronald Reagan filmed what movie at Old Tucson?

A. *The Last Outpost.*

—ψ—

Q. Who is the Arizonan known for her folk songs about cowboys?

A. Katie Lee.

Q. Where in Phoenix did actress Janet Leigh stay during the filming of the movie *Psycho*?

A. The Jefferson Hotel.

—ψ—

Q. Arizonan Travis Walton's account of his abduction by aliens was made into what 1993 movie?

A. *Fire in the Sky.*

—ψ—

Q. The annual International Film Festival and Workshop, which shows films prior to release and has filmmakers hosting question-and-answer sessions, takes place in what city?

A. Sedona.

—ψ—

Q. What Arizona locations were used for the filming of *Natural Born Killers*, starring Woody Harrelson?

A. Winslow and Holbrook.

—ψ—

Q. The movie *The Great White Hope* had what Arizona town as its setting?

A. Globe.

—ψ—

Q. The song "El Paso" was a big hit for what country music singer?

A. Marty Robbins.

—ψ—

Q. Filmed in Sedona, the movie *Johnny Guitar* had what stars?

A. Joan Crawford and Sterling Hayden.

Q. Arizona's official state balladeer, Dolan Ellis, was once a member of what musical group?

A. The New Christy Minstrels.

—ψ—

Q. Who was called the "Arizona Cowboy"?

A. Rex Allen.

—ψ—

Q. Where was the 1998 movie *The Town That Outlawed Christmas* shot?

A. Phoenix.

—ψ—

Q. What 1950s rock and roll idol who attended North Phoenix High School recorded "Plaything"?

A. Ted Newman.

—ψ—

Q. After living many years in Nashville, what country music legend moved to Arizona?

A. Waylon Jennings.

—ψ—

Q. On what location was the John Wayne movie *McClintock* filmed?

A. The San Rafael de la Zanja Ranch.

—ψ—

Q. What song sometimes identified with Arizona did Gordon Lightfoot make famous?

A. "Carefree Highway."

Q. What 1988 feature movie, starring Robert DeNiro and Charles Grodin, was filmed in locations near Globe, Flagstaff, Cameron, and Cottonwood?

A. *Midnight Run.*

—ψ—

Q. The first tequila ever produced in the United States was made in 1936 in what city?

A. Nogales.

—ψ—

Q. *Disaster at Silo 7*, starring Dennis Weaver, was filmed at what two Arizona locations?

A. Tucson and Green Valley.

—ψ—

Q. Where is the Grand Canyon Music festival held?

A. In the Shrine of the Ages Auditorium on the South Rim.

—ψ—

Q. What made-for-TV movie, featuring *Dallas* star Larry Hagman, was shot in Tucson and Page?

A. *Deadly Encounter.*

—ψ—

Q. *Dirty Dingus Magee*, a 1970 movie filmed at Old Tucson and Mescal, featured what actor/singer?

A. Frank Sinatra.

—ψ—

Q. What annual event in Chandler features ostrich racing?

A. The Chandler Ostrich Festival, held in March.

Q. Football star Joe Namath and Ann-Margaret teamed up to make what movie at Old Tucson?

A. *C. C. & Company.*

—ψ—

Q. In 1970 what TV show was filmed in Carefree?

A. *The Dick Van Dyke Show.*

—ψ—

Q. Filmed in Prescott in 1970, *Bless the Beasts and the Children* was produced and directed by what legendary moviemaker?

A. Stanley Kramer.

—ψ—

Q. Director Robert Aldrich oversaw the making of what movie made in Sedona in 1954, starring Burt Lancaster, Jean Peters, and Charles Bronson?

A. *Apache.*

—ψ—

Q. Where is the world's largest annual Native American fair held?

A. In Window Rock, in September.

—ψ—

Q. What role did Oscar-winning actor Robert Duvall play in the movie, *Geronimo*?

A. Al Sieber, an army scout during the Apache wars.

—ψ—

Q. What two Arizona locations furnished backdrops for the movie *Forrest Gump*?

A. Twin Arrows Trading Post and Monument Valley.

Q. In 1971 Bob Hope filmed what movie in Arizona?

A. *Cancel My Reservation.*

—ψ—

Q. The Lake Havasu City Yacht Club hosts an annual sailboat race in May to celebrate what historic event?

A. Mexican Independence Day.

—ψ—

Q. World War II Medal of Honor winner Audie Murphy starred in what 1956 feature that was filmed in Bear Canyon?

A. *Walk the Proud Land.*

—ψ—

Q. Where was the classic John Wayne film *The Searchers* shot?

A. Monument Valley.

—ψ—

Q. Pat Boone starred in the 1957 movie *Bernadine*, which was shot at what location?

A. Saguaro Lake.

—ψ—

Q. Each March where can visitors attend the Valley of the Sun Annual Square and Round Dance Festival?

A. Phoenix.

—ψ—

Q. The nature film *The Living Desert,* which was shot on locations all over Arizona, came from what major studio?

A. Walt Disney.

Q. Hundreds of dancers from all over the nation converge on Mesa every year in October for what huge event?

A. The Native American Powwow.

—ψ—

Q. What was Elvis Presley's first movie filmed in Arizona?

A. *Stay Away Joe*.

—ψ—

Q. Who starred in the 1981 television movie *I Married Wyatt Earp*?

A. Marie Osmond and Bruce Boxleitner.

—ψ—

Q. Jim Thorpe, the famous Native American football player, appeared in what movie in 1940?

A. *Arizona Frontier.*

—ψ—

Q. Who wrote the song "Man With the Big Hat" while he sat in Harold's Cave Creek Corral, a tavern in Cave Creek?

A. Stephen Fromholtz.

—ψ—

Q. In 1941 Robert Taylor and Brian Donlevy starred in what movie, made in Sedona and named for a murderer who killed his first victim in Arizona?

A. *Billy the Kid*.

—ψ—

Q. What Arizonan is considered by many to be the granddaddy of punk rock?

A. Alice Cooper.

Q. Country music star Dwight Yoakam co-produced what movie filmed at the Grand Canyon?

A. *Wakin' Up in Reno.*

Q. Actress Barbara Eden was born in Tucson in what year?

A. 1934.

Q. In what 1997 television movie was Cochise Stronghold near Douglas featured?

A. *The Magnificent Seven.*

Q. What award-winning 1996 movie featuring Tom Cruise and Cuba Gooding Jr. featured Sun Devil Stadium in Phoenix?

A. *Jerry Maguire.*

Q. What popular TV series broadcast several of its 1996 episodes from Payson, Phoenix, and Glendale?

A. *Unsolved Mysteries.*

Q. Entertainment for the entire family is provided by what Tuscon theater where melodramas encourage audience participation?

A. Gaslight Theatre.

Q. Filmed in Tombstone in 1994, *Wyatt Earp: Return to Tombstone* starred what actor?

A. Hugh O'Brian.

Q. Who starred in the 1993 feature film *Tombstone*?

A. Val Kilmer, Kurt Russell, and Powers Booth.

—ψ—

Q. A young Harrison Ford co-starred in what 1979 movie, filmed in Nogales and Mescal and featuring Gene Wilder?

A. *The Frisco Kid.*

—ψ—

Q. The annual Yada Yada Parade, whose motto is "the crazier the better," ends at the Antique Fair and Auction in what city?

A. Kingman.

—ψ—

Q. The television movie *The Gambler*, starring Kenny Rogers, was filmed at what Arizona location?

A. Old Tucson.

—ψ—

Q. Who produced and directed *Cheyenne Autumn*, featuring an all-star Hollywood cast and filmed in Monument Valley?

A. John Ford.

—ψ—

Q. The 1933 feature film *Robber's Roost*, starring Maureen O'Sullivan and George O'Brien, was shot at what location?

A. Oak Creek Canyon.

—ψ—

Q. Where in Arizona was *Road to Zanzibar*, with Bob Hope, Bing Crosby, and Dorothy Lamour, filmed?

A. Yuma.

Q. At what annual celebration in Tucson can one purchase chile plants while enjoying good food, music, and a variety of cultural and educational programs?

A. La Fiesta de los Chiles.

—ψ—

Q. Will Rogers Jr. lived for many years in what community?

A. Tubac.

—ψ—

Q. Shot in Old Tucson, the 1967 TV series *High Chaparral* starred what actors?

A. Leif Erickson and Cameron Mitchell.

—ψ—

Q. Some of the backdrop for the 1967 movie *Planet of the Apes*, starring Charlton Heston and Roddy McDowall, was provided by what Arizona lake?

A. Lake Powell.

—ψ—

Q. For eighty-six years a Labor Day rodeo has been held in what town?

A. Sonoita.

—ψ—

Q. Mare Winningham was born in what city on May 6, 1959?

A. Tucson.

—ψ—

Q. Who directed and starred in the 1974 movie *The Eiger Sanction*, which has scenes of Monument Valley?

A. Clint Eastwood.

Q. What legendary Hollywood figure directed the 1974 movie *Other Side of the Wind*, starring John Huston and filmed at Carefree and Cave Creek?

A. Orson Welles.

—ψ—

Q. Paul Harvey broadcasts from what site when he is in residence at his Phoenix home?

A. His own studio in his home.

—ψ—

Q. What was the first move filmed in Arizona that Gary Cooper starred in?

A. *Morocco*, in 1930.

—ψ—

Q. *Bonanza* star Pernell Roberts acted in what movie filmed in 1990 at the Phoenix International Raceway?

A. *Checkered Flag*.

—ψ—

Q. The 1986 remake of the classic movie *Stagecoach*, shot in Mescal, starred what three country music greats?

A. Waylon Jennings, Johnny Cash, and Willie Nelson.

—ψ—

Q. Who wrote the song, "Get Your Kicks on Route 66"?

A. Bobby Troup.

—ψ—

Q. In 1985 the Native American actor Will Sampson starred in what movie filmed in Canyon de Chelly?

A. *Poltergeist II: The Other Side*.

Q. Magician David Copperfield aired his TV show from what Arizona location in 1984?

A. The Grand Canyon.

Q. Luke Air Force Base was the site of the 1958 movie *The Hunters*, starring what three male actors?

A. Robert Mitchum, Robert Wagner, and Richard Egan.

Q. Mystery writer Mickey Spillane had a cameo role in what feature film shot in 1954 at the Phoenix Fairgrounds?

A. *Ring of Fear.*

Q. What trio of noted actors appeared in the 1951 movie *Fort Defiance*, filmed at Sedona?

A. Dane Clark, Ben Johnson, and Peter Graves.

Q. The annual Northern Arizona Fair is held in what town?

A. Fredonia.

Q. The legendary Humphrey Bogart, along with Lloyd Bridges, starred in what movie filmed in Yuma in 1943?

A. *Sahara.*

Q. In what town is the annual Turquoise Circuit Finals Rodeo held?

A. Bullhead City.

Q. What native of Nogales was one-half of the popular 1960s folk duet Bud and Travis?

A. Travis Edmonson.

Q. Storyteller theater and Family Carousel theater draw tourists to what Tucson attraction?

A. Old Tucson Studios.

Q. *The Red River,* starring John Wayne, was filmed along what river?

A. The San Pedro.

Q. Prescott was the birthplace of what actress on November 14, 1910?

A. Rosemary De Camp.

Q. The state's first TV station, KPHO-TV, began broadcasting in what year?

A. 1949.

Q. What Arizona location was used for the thriller movie *Seven Days in May,* starring Burt Lancaster, Kirk Douglas, Ava Gardner, and Fredric March?

A. Yuma.

Q. Where did *Gunsmoke*'s Miss Kitty once live?

A. In the Salt River Valley.

Q. In 1922 what radio station became Arizona's first licensed commercial station?

A. KFAD, now KTAR, in Phoenix.

—ψ—

Q. The annual Mining Country Boom Town Spree, featuring such competitions as drilling and mucking, takes place in April in what town?

A. Miami.

—ψ—

Q. What rocker donated $75,000 in 2001 for a new youth center in central Phoenix?

A. Alice Cooper.

—ψ—

Q. *Comanche Territory*, the 1950 feature film shot in Sedona by Paramount Studios, starred what Hollywood actors?

A. Macdonald Carey, Maureen O'Hara, and Will Geer.

—ψ—

Q. A collection of fighter airplanes from 1914 to the present may be viewed at what Mesa museum?

A. Champlin Fighter Aircraft Museum.

—ψ—

Q. Where was the 1949 movie *Lust for Gold*, starring Ida Lupino and Glenn Ford, filmed?

A. In the Superstition Mountains.

—ψ—

Q. Sedona provided the setting for what 1964 movie starring Glenn Ford and Henry Fonda?

A. *The Rounders*.

HISTORY

Q. Who was the first European to enter Arizona?

A. Francisco Vásquez de Coronado.

Q. What was Coronado looking for when he entered Arizona?

A. The fabled Seven Cities of Cibola.

Q. Friars from what order of the Catholic Church were the first to establish missions in Arizona?

A. Franciscan.

Q. Who were the Anasazi?

A. The Native American ancestors of the Pueblo peoples.

Q. Who was the first European to view the Grand Canyon?

A. Don Garcia López de Cárdenas.

Q. What Jesuit priest built twenty-nine missions, saved more than forty-eight thousand souls, and traveled thousands of miles during his missionary travels, which included Arizona?

A. Father Eusebio Francisco Kino.

Q. In what year did the Grand Canyon attain national park status?

A. 1919.

—ᛟ—

Q. Arizona became a U S. territory in what year?

A. 1863.

—ᛟ—

Q. In the order of its entry to the union, what is Arizona's rank?

A. Forty-eighth.

—ᛟ—

Q. What is Arizona's official nickname?

A. The Grand Canyon State.

—ᛟ—

Q. Other than the Grand Canyon State, what are two nicknames for Arizona?

A. The Apache State and the Copper State.

—ᛟ—

Q. Democrat Lyndon Johnson defeated what Arizonan for the presidency in 1964?

A. Barry Goldwater.

—ᛟ—

Q. The small town of Mowry grew up around silver, lead, and zinc mines, but its future became bleak when the mining operations were cut short in 1862 for what reason?

A. The owner, a Lieutenant Mowry, was charged with supplying lead for Confederate bullets.

Q. The name *Hohokam* has what meaning in the Pima Indian language?

A. "All used up."

Q. When did the Hohokam first appear as a distinct culture?

A. About 300 B.C., in the region near the juncture of the Salt and Gila Rivers.

Q. What Arizona woman became the first female justice of the U.S. Supreme Court?

A. Sandra Day O'Connor.

Q. The gunfight at the O. K. Corral took place on what date?

A. October 26, 1881.

Q. The Earp brothers had what partner in the gunfight at the O.K. Corral?

A. John H. "Doc" Holliday.

Q. What was Doc Holliday's profession?

A. Dentist.

Q. The opposing faction in the gunfight at the O. K. Corral consisted of what five men?

A. Brothers Frank and Tom McLaury, brothers Ike and Billy Clanton, and Billy Claiborne.

Q. Who is the only Arizona governor to be removed from office?

A. Evan Meacham (1987–1988).

—ψ—

Q. Their Native American foes called black soldiers in the U.S. Army fighting in the West by what name?

A. Buffalo soldiers.

—ψ—

Q. What were the four regiments of buffalo soldiers, many of whose members served in the Arizona Territory?

A. The Ninth and Tenth Cavalry and the Twenty-fourth and Twenty-fifth Infantry Regiments.

—ψ—

Q. Who commanded the Tenth Cavalry Regiment of buffalo soldiers?

A. Col. Benjamin H. Grierson (a white officer).

—ψ—

Q. The conquistadors compared the Grand Canyon with what building back home in Spain?

A. The Great Tower at Seville.

—ψ—

Q. For whom was the city of Sedona named?

A. Pioneer woman Sedona Schnebly.

—ψ—

Q. What noted American explorer, called the "Pathfinder of the West," became Arizona's territorial governor in 1878?

A. John C. Frémont.

Q. What was the first U.S. college located on an Indian reservation?

A. Navajo Community College, in Tsaile, in 1969.

—ψ—

Q. Billy the Kid's first murder victim was what Arizonan?

A. Frank P. Cahill.

—ψ—

Q. Where did Billy the Kid kill Frank Cahill?

A. At Camp Grant, a U.S. Army post situated in the southeastern part of the Arizona Territory.

—ψ—

Q. After state supreme court justices are appointed by the governor and serve a six-year term, how do they continue service?

A. Voters vote yes or no as to whether they should retain their seat on the bench.

—ψ—

Q. What cabinet-level position did Arizonan Stewart Udall hold during the administrations of Presidents John F. Kennedy and Lyndon B. Johnson?

A. Secretary of the Interior.

—ψ—

Q. For how many years did Barry Goldwater serve as U.S. senator?

A. Thirty.

—ψ—

Q. The land that became Arizona came under the rule of Mexico in what year, when that country won its independence from Spain?

A. 1821.

Q. When was the Pueblo Revolt, an uprising that sent the Spanish back into Mexico?

A. 1680.

—ψ—

Q. Who was the first woman to become governor of Arizona?

A. Rose Mofford (1988–1991).

—ψ—

Q. When was the first permanent white settlement in Arizona begun?

A. In 1752, near Tubac.

—ψ—

Q. In 1853 what transaction with Mexico added the region south of the Gila River, in present-day Arizona and New Mexico, to form the present boundary of the United States?

A. The Gadsden Purchase ($10 million for 29,640 square miles).

—ψ—

Q. For what political act is territorial governor John C. Frémont best known?

A. He was the first presidential candidate to run on the Republican Party ticket, losing to James Buchanan in 1856.

—ψ—

Q. Bruce Babbitt, governor from 1978 to 1987, went on to serve in what U.S. cabinet position?

A. Secretary of the Interior, under Bill Clinton.

—ψ—

Q. When was Arizona's original constitution adopted?

A. 1911.

Q. What early photographer had studios next door to the O. K. Corral?

A. C. S. Fly.

—ψ—

Q. Who was the Arizona Territory's last governor?

A. Richard E. Sloan (1909–1911).

—ψ—

Q. For the state of Arizona, what were the percentages of the popular vote for each candidate in the Barry Goldwater/Lyndon Johnson presidential race of 1964?

A. Goldwater, 50.5 percent; Johnson, 49.5 percent.

—ψ—

Q. In what city is the Arizona Historical Society Museum located?

A. Tucson.

—ψ—

Q. In 1850 what incident turned Geronimo into the leader of the Apache resistance?

A. His mother, wife, and three children were murdered by white men.

—ψ—

Q. John C. Frémont received what salary as Arizona's territorial governor?

A. Twenty-six hundred dollars per year.

—ψ—

Q. Under what circumstances did Governor Frémont leave office?

A. He was forced to resign, primarily because of his perpetual absence from Arizona.

Q. After Kit Carson besieged Canyon de Chelly in 1864, eight thousand Navajos were moved to the New Mexico Territory on a forced march commonly called by what name?

A. The Long Walk.

—ψ—

Q. Communities of what size may vote to incorporate as a city or town?

A. Fifteen hundred people.

—ψ—

Q. For whom was the frontier post Fort Whipple named?

A. Lt. Amiel Weeks Whipple, a U.S. army topographical engineer.

—ψ—

Q. Arizona's first library was probably the library established in Arivaca in the 1860s by what man?

A. Samuel Colt, the pistol maker, who had a mine in Arivaca and provided books for his workers.

—ψ—

Q. In 1899, in what may have been the last true stagecoach heist, what female outlaw robbed the Benson-to-Globe stagecoach in 1899?

A. Pearl Hart.

—ψ—

Q. What two buffalo soldiers were awarded the Medal of Honor for their valor at Cedar Springs, Arizona Territory, in 1889?

A. Sgt. Benjamin Brown and Cpl. Isaiah Mays.

—ψ—

Q. In what year were Native Americans in Arizona allowed to vote?

A. 1948.

Q. What Phoenix aviator shot down at least four German airplanes and fifteen balloons during World War I, a feat for which he was awarded the Medal of Honor?

A. Frank Luke.

Q. How many Arizonans have been awarded the Medal of Honor by the army, navy, or marines?

A. Twenty-one.

Q. When was the first cotton grown by white settlers in Arizona?

A. In 1873, near Phoenix.

Q. Maj. John Wesley Powell, the leader of the first exploration of the Grand Canyon, had what physical disability?

A. He had lost one arm at the battle of Shiloh during the Civil War.

Q. For what purpose did the Spanish build Tucson in the late 1700s?

A. To serve as a *presidio*, or armed outpost, to protect the northern frontier from marauding Indians.

Q. What ancient people were the ancestors of the Apache and Navajo?

A. Athapaskan.

Q. What was the major occupation of some early Americans, called mountain men, who frequented the West during the 1820s?

A. Fur trapping.

Q. Carl Hayden served how many continuous years in the U.S. Congress?

A. Fifty-six.

—ψ—

Q. Coconino County's name means what in the Havasupai language?

A. "Little water."

—ψ—

Q. What are the three principal industries of the state's plateau region?

A. Livestock raising, lumbering, and tourism.

—ψ—

Q. The Southern Pacific Railroad connected Yuma and Tucson in what year?

A. 1880.

—ψ—

Q. The roots of the Arizona Historical Society extend back to what organization formed in 1884?

A. Society of Arizona Pioneers, started by a group of Tucson citizens.

—ψ—

Q. The so-called Pleasant Valley War in 1887, between cattle and sheep factions, involved what two families?

A. Tewksbury and Graham.

—ψ—

Q. According to the 2000 census, the state's population increased by 40 percent in the past decade, with what three counties having the largest per capita gains?

A. Maricopa, Pima, and Yuma.

Q. From what Arizona community does Justice Sandra Day O'Connor hail?

A. Duncan.

_ψ_

Q. With a growth rate of 40 percent, how does Arizona rank among the states in fastest growth rate?

A. Second, behind Nevada's 66 percent.

_ψ_

Q. A member of the Rough Riders, what former mayor of Prescott was killed in action in Cuba during the Spanish-American War?

A. William O. "Buckey" O'Neill.

_ψ_

Q. The present Department of Library, Archives, and Public Records evolved from what institution founded in 1864?

A. Arizona Territorial Library.

_ψ_

Q. More than forty cities, including most of the largest ones, have what type of city government?

A. City manager.

_ψ_

Q. What federal territory was Arizona originally part of?

A. The Territory of New Mexico.

_ψ_

Q. In 1919 what city became the first in the nation to have its own municipal airport?

A. Tucson.

Q. Under the present rules, how many terms may the governor serve?

A. Any number but no more than two consecutive terms.

—ψ—

Q. If a sitting governor dies or resigns, by whom is he or she succeeded?

A. One of the four elected state officials, in order of succession: secretary of state, attorney general, state treasurer, superintendent of public instruction.

—ψ—

Q. In 1863 why did President Abraham Lincoln create the separate Territory of Arizona?

A. To counter the creation of the Confederate Territory of Arizona.

—ψ—

Q. In 1877 what was the first railroad to enter the region?

A. Southern Pacific, when it built its line into Yuma.

—ψ—

Q. In the 1890s what was considered the rowdiest silver camp between Globe and Virginia City, while in six years its fifteen mines produced $12 million in silver bullion?

A. White Hills, fifty miles north of Kingman in Mohave County.

—ψ—

Q. What U. S. president vetoed the Arizona statehood bill in 1911?

A. William Howard Taft.

—ψ—

Q. In what year did the Atlantic and Pacific Railroad cross Arizona?

A. 1883.

Q. What are the state senatorial and representative terms of office?

A. Two years.

Q. What national calamity closed nearly all of Arizona's copper mines between 1931 and 1934?

A. The Great Depression.

Q. When did Arizona pass its "right to work" amendment to the state constitution?

A. 1946.

Q. In 1988 what governor was impeached, convicted, and removed from office?

A. Evan Meacham, for illegally lending state money to his automobile dealership and trying to block an investigation.

Q. When Governor Meacham was removed from office, what secretary of state automatically succeeded him?

A. Rose Mofford, thus becoming Arizona's first woman governor.

Q. What caused the infamous Camp Grant Massacre of 1871?

A. Trumped up charges of Indian raids in the area caused some of Tucson's leading citizens to murder more than one hundred Apaches, mostly women and children.

Q. In the 1950s what were Tucson's main tourist attractions?

A. Dude ranches.

Q. Arizona was admitted to the union on what date?

A. February 14, 1912.

— ψ —

Q. The Arizona legislature contains how many senators and representatives?

A. Thirty senators and sixty representatives.

— ψ —

Q. Elected in 1975, who was the first Hispanic governor of Arizona?

A. Raul Castro.

— ψ —

Q. How many men served as territorial governors?

A. Sixteen, with one, Nathan O. Murphy, serving twice.

— ψ —

Q. As a result of the 2000 census, Arizona increased its electoral college representation to what number?

A. Ten, compared to eight by the 1990 census.

— ψ —

Q. In 1884 what former sheriff of Tombstone purchased the San Bernardino Ranch in Cochise County and turned it into a prize cattle-raising facility?

A. John Slaughter.

— ψ —

Q. According to the 2000 census, what was the fastest growing town in Arizona?

A. Lukachukai in Navajo Nation, which grew 1,284 percent, for a total of 1,565.

Q. What is the nickname for the town of Tombstone?

A. "The Town Too Tough to Die."

—ψ—

Q. The Grand Canyon Lodge was built by what organization?

A. The Union Pacific Railroad.

—ψ—

Q. What years did George W. P. Hunt, the state's first governor, serve?

A. 1912–1919, 1923–1929, 1931–1933.

—ψ—

Q. The first woman in the United States to head a state supreme court was what Arizonan?

A. Judge Lorna Lockwood, elected chief justice of the Arizona Supreme Court in 1965.

—ψ—

Q. Now included in Pipe Spring National Monument, what did the Mormon leader Brigham Young have built to protect travelers from the Indians?

A. A fort called Winsor Castle.

—ψ—

Q. At the end of the Civil War, how many U. S. military posts were situated in the Arizona Territory?

A. Fourteen.

—ψ—

Q. At the turn of the last century, who was called the "cattle king of Arizona?"

A. Col. Henry C. Hooker.

Q. Who was Arizona's first territorial governor?

A. John N. Goodwin (1863–1866).

Q. What Phoenix resident was awarded both the Army and Navy Medals of Honor for his valorous service in World War I?

A. Cpl. John Henry Pruitt of the U.S. Marine Corps.

Q. Of the seventeen Arizona residents receiving the Army Medal of Honor, how many were Native Americans who were awarded their honors for bravery while serving as scouts for the U.S. Army?

A. Eleven.

Q. Counties are governed by what officials?

A. A three- or five-member board of supervisors.

Q. What does the Coronado National Memorial in Cochise County commemorate?

A. The first major European exploration of the Southwest.

Q. What order of the Catholic Church founded the mission of San Jose de Tumacacori, between Tucson and Nogales?

A. The Jesuits.

Q. During the 1530s what Spanish explorer wandered across the southern part of Arizona while trying to find his way back to Mexico after a shipwreck in the Gulf of Mexico?

A. Cabeza de Vaca.

Q. Whom did Barry Goldwater defeat in the 1952 U.S. senate race?

A. Ernest W. McFarland.

—ψ—

Q. Which military post in Arizona was named for a pre–Civil War U.S. president?

A. Fort Buchanan, named for President James Buchanan.

—ψ—

Q. What were the first names of the Earp brothers who participated in the gunfight at the O. K. Corral?

A. Wyatt, Virgil, and Morgan.

—ψ—

Q. What strategic pass in the Chiricahua Mountains did Fort Bowie protect?

A. Apache.

—ψ—

Q. According to the 2000 census, Arizona had how many people per square mile?

A. Forty-five.

—ψ—

Q. Why was Fort Bowie important from the late 1860s to the 1880s?

A. It was the center for army operations against the Apaches led by Geronimo, Cochise, and Natchez.

—ψ—

Q. When Barry Goldwater's grandfather first went to the West, what was his occupation?

A. Peddler in the gold camps (he was a recent immigrant).

Q. What president appointed Sandra Day O'Connor to the U.S. Supreme Court?

A. Ronald Reagan.

Q. What U.S. president restored the original name of Hoover to what by then had become known as Boulder Dam?

A. President Harry Truman, in 1947.

Q. Who is thought to be the first white settler in Arizona to build a ranch house?

A. Pete Kitchen, in 1853.

—ψ—

Q. Besides its fame as a mining town, of what commercial superlative did Jerome once boast?

A. It had the largest J. C. Penney store in Arizona.

—ψ—

Q. For what type of ore was the region around Bisbee famous?

A. Copper.

—ψ—

Q. In 1966 what Phoenix warehouse worker, who confessed to charges of kidnapping and rape, had a major impact on the nation's law enforcement operations?

A. Ernesto A. Miranda, causing the U.S. Supreme Court decision in *Miranda* v. *Arizona*.

—ψ—

Q. When was the first book printed in Arizona?

A. 1860.

Q. When the last of the Hubbell family died in 1957, what became of the eighty-year-old Hubbell Trading Post, which did business with the Navajo Indians?

A. It was purchased by the federal government and declared a national historic site.

Q. What is Tucson's nickname?

A. "The Old Pueblo."

Q. Between the 1990 and the 2000 censuses, by what percentage did Arizona's Hispanic population grow?

A. 80 percent.

Q. What Native American was the first Indian commissioner for the U.S. government?

A. Ely Parker.

Q. When was the battleship USS *Arizona* destroyed?

A. December 7, 1941, at Pearl Harbor.

—ψ—

Q. What was Tombstone's original name?

A. Goose Flats.

—ψ—

Q. Where did Arizona's largest Civil War battle take place?

A. At Picacho Peak, near Casa Grande.

Q. An underground or partly underground chamber in a Pueblo village, used by the men for ceremonies or councils, is called what?

A. A kiva.

—ψ—

Q. During World War II members of what Arizona tribe transmitted military messages for the U.S. Army in their native tongue, which the Japanese were unable to translate?

A. The Navajo.

—ψ—

Q. For whom was the town of Clifton named?

A. Henry Clifton, an early prospector.

—ψ—

Q. When was the Grand Canyon Lodge built?

A. 1928.

—ψ—

Q. In 1910 why did President William Howard Taft veto the bill permitting Arizona to draw up a constitution and apply for statehood?

A. The constitution allowed voters to recall judges from office. (After the clause was removed and Arizona became a state, the constitution was changed to permit recall.)

—ψ—

Q. As of 2001, how many governors have served the state of Arizona?

A. Twenty-two.

—ψ—

Q. What was the original size of the Hopi Indian Reservation?

A. 2,472,320 acres; it is now 1,542,306 acres.

Q. What Native American of the Pima tribe became famous when he helped raise the American flag on Iwo Jima?

A. Ira Hayes.

—ψ—

Q. Jessie, the daughter of the powerful senator from Missouri, Thomas Hart Benton, married what flamboyant figure associated with Arizona history?

A. John C. Frémont.

—ψ—

Q. When did Jane Dee Hull become governor of Arizona?

A. 1997.

—ψ—

Q. Four times since 1950 the National Civic League has selected Phoenix for what honor?

A. An All-American City.

—ψ—

Q. What U.S. senator from Arizona, a former Vietnam War POW, sought the Republican nomination for president in 2000?

A. John McCain.

—ψ—

Q. What Arizonan was the first Chinese-American in the U.S. to be elected to a state legislature?

A. Wing Ong of Phoenix, in 1966.

—ψ—

Q. Prospector and restaurant owner Nellie Cashman was known by what nickname?

A. "Angel of the Mining Camps."

Q. "The West's Most Western Town" refers to what Arizona city?

A. Scottsdale.

Q. Where and when was Arizona's worst air tragedy?

A. The Grand Canyon in 1956, when 128 people were killed.

Q. As one of four states gaining two seats in Congress as a result of the 2000 census, how many representatives will Arizona have after the 2002 election?

A. Eight (the other states are Texas, Florida, and Georgia).

Q. Martin Luther King Day became an official holiday in Arizona in what year?

A. 1996.

Q. Who is the only governor of Arizona ever to resign the office?

A. Fife Symington (1991–1997).

Q. What was the origin of the town of Camp Verde?

A. Founded in 1866 as Camp Lincoln by Arizona Volunteers to keep the Apache at bay, it later became a U.S. Army post called Fort Verde.

Q. To what town did the territorial prison at Yuma move in 1909?

A. Florence.

Q. Who brought the first cattle into the area that became Arizona?

A. Father Eusebio Francisco Kino.

—ψ—

Q. What perennial presidential candidate and later U.S. secretary of state visited Phoenix on the day in 1912 when Arizona attained statehood?

A. William Jennings Bryan.

—ψ—

Q. What radio personality later became mayor of Phoenix in 1956 and governor in 1967?

A. Jack Williams.

—ψ—

Q. Who nominated Barry Goldwater for president at the 1964 Republican convention?

A. Ronald Reagan.

—ψ—

Q. Who was the first U.S. president to visit Arizona?

A. William McKinley, in 1901.

—ψ—

Q. In 1997 why was Gov. Fife Symington forced to resign as governor?

A. He had been convicted of fraud earlier that year when he had been a real estate developer, and state law required his resignation.

—ψ—

Q. What general, born at Fort Huachuca, commanded U.S. forces at Guadalcanal in the South Pacific in 1942?

A. Alexander McCarrell Patch Jr.

Q. Who was the first black person to set foot on the land that became Arizona?

A. Estevanico (Esteban), a slave from Morocco who in 1539 was with Marcos de Niza's exploratory party. He was sent ahead to seek information and was killed by the Zuni.

Q. What city started a rental library in the 1870s?

A. Tucson (Phoenix and Prescott had small libraries by 1878).

Q. How does Arizona rank nationally in per pupil total expenditures in the public schools?

A. Forty-eighth ($4,476 per pupil compared to first place New Jersey with $9,361, according to 1995–1996 figures).

Q. Former New York mayor Fiorello La Guardia spent much of his youth in what Arizona town?

A. Prescott.

Q. Nicknamed "Double Glasses," who was the founder of Hubbell's Trading Post?

A. Lorenzo Hubbell.

Q. When was the construction of the Arizona capitol completed?

A. 1901, while the area was still a territory.

Q. When was statehood first proposed for Arizona?

A. 1892.

Q. Who was the first African American elected to the Arizona legislature?

A. Clovis Campbell, in 1966.

—ψ—

Q. What people were the first in the Americas to utilize irrigation?

A. The Hohokam of Arizona and New Mexico.

—ψ—

Q. In the 1960s what proposal jeopardized the Grand Canyon?

A. Construction of two high dams for the Colorado River.

—ψ—

Q. What schoolteacher from Tennessee passed through the town of Tubac in 1849 on his way to the California gold fields and found the place deserted?

A. Benjamin Butler Harris.

—ψ—

Q. What army general is credited with Geronimo's final defeat?

A. General Nelson A. Miles.

—ψ—

Q. What distinction did General Miles have later in his career?

A. He became commander-in-chief of the U. S. Army in 1900.

—ψ—

Q. In 1540, when Spanish explorer Francisco Vasquéz de Coronado came to the region searching for the wondrous golden cities, what did he find?

A. Zuni pueblos that shone like gold in the sunlight.

Q. In 1827 what famous mountain man lost half of his trapping party to Mohave Indians, an incident known as the Mohave Massacre?

A. Jedediah Smith.

—ψ—

Q. Who led the U.S. Army's survey of the proposed transcontinental railroad route through present-day Arizona in 1853?

A. Lt. Amiel Whipple.

—ψ—

Q. After the Mexican War what American diplomat negotiated with Mexico to purchase a strip of land south of the Gila River?

A. James Gadsden.

—ψ—

Q. Who was the Dutchman of the Lost Dutchman Mine fame?

A. Jacob Waltz.

—ψ—

Q. Barry Goldwater carried what six states in the 1964 presidential election?

A. Arizona, Alabama, Georgia, Louisiana, Mississippi, and South Carolina.

—ψ—

Q. The Butterfield Overland Mail followed what route in Arizona?

A. The Gila Trail, a wagon trail blazed earlier by Col. Philip St. George Cooke.

—ψ—

Q. What service replaced the Overland Mail?

A. The Pony Express, from April 1860 until October 1861.

Q. Why did the Pony Express last only eighteen months?

A. There was no more need for it, as the telegraph then spanned the continent.

Q. In 1862 who marched into Tucson at the head of two hundred Confederate soldiers?

A. Capt. Sherrod Hunter.

Q. What battle in New Mexico in 1862 spelled the doom of the Confederate presence in the Southwest?

A. Glorieta Pass, sometimes called the "Gettysburg of the West."

Q. In 1862, as commander of the Department of New Mexico, which included Arizona, what Union general held the unruly territory under harsh martial law?

A. James Henry Carlton.

Q. What were the names of the three rowboats used in 1871 on the second Powell expedition down the Colorado River?

A. *Emma Dean, Nellie Powell,* and *Canonita.*

Q. For whom was the ghost town of McMillenville, located in Gila County, named?

A. Charles McMillen, a local prospector.

Q. How old was Geronimo when he died?

A. Eighty-six.

Q. The first white person known to have entered the Arizona region was what Franciscan priest?

A. Marcos de Niza, who traveled through San Pedro Valley in 1539 looking for the fabled Seven Cities of Cibola that were supposed to be made of gold.

—ψ—

Q. In 1992 Willie Wong, Arizona's first Asian American mayor, was elected in what city?

A. Mesa.

—ψ—

Q. Governor, U.S. senator, and chief justice of the Arizona Supreme Court all apply to what Arizonan?

A. Ernest W. McFarland.

—ψ—

Q. Who was Arizona's first female U.S. representative?

A. Isabella S. Greenway.

—ψ—

Q. To curtail cattle rustling, in 1901 what group was established?

A. Arizona Rangers.

—ψ—

Q. Who was the founder of Phoenix?

A. Jack Swilling, a prospector from Wickenburg.

—ψ—

Q. How many men from Arizona volunteered to serve in Theodore Roosevelt's Rough Riders in the Spanish-American War?

A. 203 officers and men.

Q. Who commanded the Arizona contingent in the Rough Riders?

A. Maj. Alexander O. Brodie.

Q. After the Spanish-American War, what political position did Maj. Alexander Brodie hold?

A. Governor of Arizona Territory, appointed by President Theodore Roosevelt.

Q. How many separate tribes of Apaches were there?

A. Six.

Q. Apache leaders Cochise, Geronimo, Victorio, Nana, and Mangas Colorados were all members of what Apache tribe?

A. Chiricahua.

Q. What was the location of the 1861 incident known as the Bascom Affair, in which the inexperienced Lt. George Bascom of the U.S. Army tried to capture Cochise, the leader of the Apaches, leading to a long series of wars with the Apaches?

A. Apache Pass.

Q. Who is generally credited with giving Phoenix its name?

A. Darrel Duppa, an adventurer from England.

Q. Why was the city named Phoenix?

A. As a new city, people predicted, it would rise from the site of a vanished civilization, as the mythical bird rose from its ashes.

Q. The 1880 census shows 850 people of what ethnic background living in Pima County and enumerated as "railroad workers"?

A. Chinese.

＿ψ＿

Q. Gordon Liddy of Watergate notoriety, cartoonist Bil Keane, and hotelier Leona Helmsley have what in common?

A. They are all Arizona residents.

＿ψ＿

Q. In the 1880s at the toll gate at Central and McDowell Avenues in Phoenix bicycles were admitted free but what did the owner, the Central Avenue Improvement Association, charge for buggies and wagons?

A. Twenty-five cents.

＿ψ＿

Q. The state's first public school opened in Tucson in what year?

A. 1871.

＿ψ＿

Q. Because of its penchant for lawlessness, Tombstone was threatened with martial law in May 1882, by what U.S. president?

A. Chester A. Arthur.

＿ψ＿

Q. When did the Cochise County seat move from Tombstone to Bisbee?

A. 1929.

＿ψ＿

Q. What city in the state has the highest percentage of Asian population?

A. Tempe, with 4.7 percent.

Q. In what Mormon state, proposed by church leader Brigham Young, was most of present-day Arizona to be?

A. Deseret.

—ψ—

Q. How did John C. Frémont's gubernatorial career end?

A. He resigned under criticism in 1881.

—ψ—

Q. Who has been described as "the preeminent historian of Arizona"?

A. James Harvey McClintock.

—ψ—

Q. James H. McClintock held what military position during the Spanish-American War?

A. Captain, commanding Arizona troops of the First U.S. Volunteer Cavalry (Rough Riders).

—ψ—

Q. What political appointment did James Harvey McClintock hold in later life?

A. Postmaster of Phoenix (1902–1914 and 1928–1933).

—ψ—

Q. How old was John H. "Doc" Holliday when he died of tuberculosis in 1887?

A. Thirty-six.

—ψ—

Q. What happened to "Doc" Holliday's widow, Kate?

A. She remarried and ran a boarding house in Globe.

Q. When he died in 1972, Sen. Carl Hayden held what honorary post?

A. President pro tempore of the U.S. Senate.

—ψ—

Q. In 1872 who directed that a ferry crossing be built across the Colorado River at Marble Canyon?

A. Brigham Young.

—ψ—

Q. Who operated the first ferry across the Colorado River?

A. John D. Lee.

—ψ—

Q. When was Navajo Bridge built over the Colorado River at Marble Canyon?

A. 1928.

—ψ—

Q. In 1857 what U.S. secretary of war championed a thirty-thousand-dollar experiment to use camels as beasts of burden in the American Southwest?

A. Jefferson Davis, soon to be president of the Confederate States of America.

ARTS & LITERATURE

C H A P T E R   F O U R

Q. What writer and political activist whose novels concern the strength and endurance of poor and disenfranchised people of the Southwest wrote *The Bean Trees*?

A. Barbara Kingsolver.

Q. Historian William H. Prescott, for whom the city was named, wrote what two classics about the conquest of countries?

A. *The Conquest of Mexico* and *The Conquest of Peru*.

Q. Who was the author of *Roadside Arizona?*

A. Marshall Trimble.

Q. What Tucson resident in 1963 was awarded the Levi Strauss Saddleman Award by the Western Writers of America for lifetime achievement in preserving the history, legends, and literature of the American West?

A. Fred Grove.

Q. What award-winning writer and poet spends his time between homes in Alpine and Oracle?

A. John Duncklee.

Q. The fine production of art, nature, and photography books is the specialty of what Flagstaff publishing company?

A. Northland Publishing.

—ψ—

Q. When did Reginald W. Manning of the *Arizona Republic* win the Pulitzer Prize for editorial cartooning?

A. 1951.

—ψ—

Q. What book, published in 1875, told of Maj. John Wesley Powell's adventures through the Grand Canyon?

A. *Explorations of the Colorado River of the West and Its Tributaries.*

—ψ—

Q. Running the survey to establish the border between the United States and Mexico in the early 1850s was what former bookstore owner?

A. John Russell Bartlett.

—ψ—

Q. *Back to Bisbee* was written by what author?

A. Richard Shelton.

—ψ—

Q. When did the first college on an Arizona Indian reservation open for business?

A. 1969 (The Navajo Community College at Tsaile).

—ψ—

Q. What Scottsdale author wrote *Bless the Beasts and the Children, The Homesman,* and *They Came to Cordura*?

A. Glendon Swarthout.

Q. Glendon Swarthout received what award in 1991 from the Western Writers of America?

A. Owen Wister Award for Lifetime Achievement.

—ψ—

Q. With three thousand graduate and undergraduate students, what is Arizona's only private Christian liberal arts university?

A. Grand Canyon University.

—ψ—

Q. Volumes about the life and legends of his town are written by what Tombstone resident?

A. Ben Traywick.

—ψ—

Q. What writer from Portal is known for her juvenile and young adult novels?

A. Jeanne Williams.

—ψ—

Q. A resident of Lake Havasu City, what author writes novels of the American West?

A. Gary McCarthy.

—ψ—

Q. When did Zane Grey first travel to Arizona?

A. 1907.

—ψ—

Q. In what year did Rita Dove of Arizona State University win the Pulitzer Prize for poetry?

A. 1967.

Q. Rita Dove's Pulitzer Prize was for what book of poetry?

A. *Thomas and Beulah.*

—ψ—

Q. What is Arizona's official song?

A. "Arizona March Song," by Margaret Rowe Clifford and Maurice Blumenthal.

—ψ—

Q. What song by Rex Allen is sometimes referred to as the state song?

A. "Arizona."

—ψ—

Q. What is the state motto?

A. *Ditat Deus* ("God enriches").

—ψ—

Q. What artists' group was founded in a bar in Sedona?

A. Cowboy Artists of America (CAA).

—ψ—

Q. Who is the official balladeer of Arizona?

A. Dolan Ellis.

—ψ—

Q. Now a national historical landmark, what winter home did architect Frank Lloyd Wright build in Scottsdale?

A. Taliesin West.

Q. During World War II what two-time Pulitzer Prize–winning cartoonist created the GI characters Willie and Joe?

A. Bill Mauldin, from Phoenix.

—ψ—

Q. Although he is a New Mexican novelist, what writer often uses Navajoland as the locale for his books?

A. Tony Hillerman.

—ψ—

Q. Where can one visit the Heard Museum of Anthropology and Primitive Art?

A. Phoenix.

—ψ—

Q. Who wrote *A River No More: The Colorado River and the West*?

A. Philip L. Fradkin.

—ψ—

Q. What architect designed Gammage Memorial Auditorium at Arizona State University?

A. Frank Lloyd Wright.

—ψ—

Q. Andy Devine memorabilia is housed in a room in what museum?

A. The Mohave Museum of History and Arts, in Kingman.

—ψ—

Q. During the early 1900s what brothers ran a photographic studio on the South Rim of the Grand Canyon?

A. The Kolb brothers.

Q. Who wrote *It Happened in Arizona?*

A. James A. Crutchfield.

—ψ—

Q. Where is the Arizona Historical Society Pioneer Museum located?

A. Flagstaff.

—ψ—

Q. What was the former use of the building in which this museum is housed?

A. A hospital for the poor.

—ψ—

Q. What is unique about the construction of this building?

A. It is made from volcanic rock.

—ψ—

Q. What museum near Chandler houses a collection of rare Gila baskets?

A. Gila River Arts and Crafts Center.

—ψ—

Q. In 1983 how did the U.S. Senate honor Eve Ball for her writings about Native Americans in the Southwest?

A. It adopted a resolution recognizing her work and thanking her for "the invaluable legacy such writings will be for future generations."

—ψ—

Q. Phoenix's Orpheum Theatre is built in what style of architecture?

A. Spanish Revival.

Q. What Phoenix architect designed the Burton Barr Central Phoenix Public Library, which opened in 1995?

A. William Bruder.

—ψ—

Q. Why is Phoenix's Pueblo Grande Museum designated a national historic landmark?

A. It contains a prehistoric Hohokam village ruin.

—ψ—

Q. What was Zane Grey's real name?

A. Pearl Grey.

—ψ—

Q. The home of what nineteenth-century riverboat operator is the centerpiece for the Yuma Crossing State Historic Park?

A. Capt. G. A. Johnson.

—ψ—

Q. Between 1930 and 1945 who built Mystery Castle in Phoenix?

A. Boyce Gulley.

—ψ—

Q. Tucson's Saint Augustine Cathedral is modeled after what church in Mexico?

A. The Cathedral of Querataro.

—ψ—

Q. Founded in 1885 as the state's first institution of higher learning, the University of Arizona has a campus covering how many acres?

A. 352.

Q. What is the enrollment of the University of Arizona?

A. 34,326.

—ψ—

Q. From whom did the Navajo learn the art of silversmithing?

A. The Spanish.

—ψ—

Q. What is the region's oldest and largest anthropology museum?

A. The Arizona State Museum in Tucson, organized in 1893.

—ψ—

Q. Where is America's largest Native American ceremonial structure?

A. Casa Malpais Archaeological Park in Springerville.

—ψ—

Q. The American Graduate School of International Management is in what city?

A. Glendale.

—ψ—

Q. How many Christmas lights are used in the annual Red Rock Fantasy of Lights display at Sedona?

A. Approximately one million.

—ψ—

Q. What Tucson resident is the American author best known for science fiction that blends social criticism with awareness of runaway technology?

A. Ray Bradbury.

Q. Upon what is Colin Fletcher's book *The Man Who Walked Through Time* based?

A. The author's hikes in the Grand Canyon.

—ψ—

Q. What novelist and essayist won immediate fame with her first book, *The Land of Little Rain*, which described desert life?

A. Mary Austin.

—ψ—

Q. In *Apache Gold and Yaqui Silver*, what does the author, J. Frank Dobie, describe?

A. Lost mines.

—ψ—

Q. Who wrote *The Book of the Hopi*?

A. Frank Waters.

—ψ—

Q. Noted for her humor, what syndicated columnist who lived in Paradise Valley wrote such works as *The Grass Is Always Greener over the Septic Tank*?

A. Erma Bombeck.

—ψ—

Q. What magazine published in Arizona has an international reputation and circulation?

A. *Arizona Highways.*

—ψ—

Q. What staffer for the *Arizona Republic* was awarded the Pulitzer Prize for editorial cartooning in 1993?

A. Steve Benson.

Q. What Englishman came to Arizona in the 1880s, became a cowboy, and later designed several observatories in the state?

A. Godfrey Sykes.

Q. Who compiled the helpful guide *Arizona Place Names*?

A. Will Croft Barnes.

Q. What Arizona newspaper has been in continuous publication since May 1, 1880?

A. The *Tombstone Epitaph*.

Q. Who wrote *The Monkey Wrench Gang* about a group of environmental guerrillas?

A. Edward Abbey.

Q. Where did Edward Abbey die?

A. In Oracle.

Q. What two books did Frederick Dellenbaugh write about his Grand Canyon experiences with the Powell expedition?

A. *Romance of the Colorado River* and *A Canyon Voyage*.

Q. Frederick Dellenbaugh was a founder of what exclusive organization?

A. The Explorers' Club.

Q. Who wrote *Zane Grey's Arizona*, published in 1984?

A. Candace C. Kant.

—ψ—

Q. William H. Robinson wrote what novel set in the Choya Valley during the 1890s?

A. *Thirsty Earth.*

—ψ—

Q. What Globe resident penned the book *Cowboy*?

A. Ross Santee.

—ψ—

Q. Mary Kidder Rak wrote what two books in the 1930s depicting ranch life in Cochise County?

A. *A Cowman's Wife* and *Mountain Cattle.*

—ψ—

Q. Who was the author of *Coronado's Quest*?

A. Grove Day.

—ψ—

Q. What army engineer wrote *Report upon the Colorado River of the West*, published in 1861?

A. Lt. Joseph C. Ives.

—ψ—

Q. What Arizona institution sponsors one of the world's largest photographic museums?

A. The University of Arizona (Center for Creative Photography).

Q. How many photographs are available for viewing at the Center for Creative Photography?

A. Sixty thousand.

Q. Who was the founder and first publisher of the *Tombstone Epitaph*?

A. John P. Clum.

Q. What type of art does the Phippen Museum in Prescott feature?

A. Past and contemporary art.

Q. What western artist founded and was the first president of Cowboy Artists of America (CAA)?

A. George Phippen.

Q. What was the name of Barry Goldwater's home in Phoenix?

A. Be-Nun-I-Kin, meaning "house on the hill" in Navajo.

Q. Where may one enjoy a collection of antique dolls, toys, and model trains, as well as restored automobiles?

A. Golden Era Toy and Auto Museum, in Coolidge.

Q. What hotel in Douglas features a Tiffany mural made from stained glass?

A. The Gadsden.

Q. Flagstaff is home to what college?

A. Northern Arizona University (NAU).

—ψ—

Q. What semiannual sale features Navajo and Hopi arts and crafts?

A. The Native American Art Auction at Ganado.

—ψ—

Q. Before he became a writer, what profession did Zane Grey follow?

A. Dentistry.

—ψ—

Q. Who wrote *Wyatt Earp: Frontier Marshal*?

A. Stuart N. Lake.

—ψ—

Q. For what is Bisbee best known today?

A. As a cultural center for artists, dancers, writers, musicians, and photographers.

—ψ—

Q. What 1998 book by Stephen J. Pyne traces the history of the Grand Canyon?

A. *How the Canyon Became Grand.*

—ψ—

Q. What account of the construction of Boulder Dam won its author, Joseph Stevens, a Spur Award from the Western Writers of America in 1988?

A. *Hoover Dam: An American Adventure.*

Q. What Tucson resident was a founder and first president of the Western Writers of America?

A. Nelson Nye.

Q. What Arizona county courthouse was built in 1927 in the Spanish Colonial architectural style?

A. Pima in Tucson.

Q. What is Tucson's oldest historical district called?

A. Armory Park.

Q. For whom was the El Tovar Hotel named?

A. The Spanish explorer Pedro de Tovar.

Q. What three styles of architecture are prevalent in Flagstaff's historic downtown district?

A. Victorian, Tudor Revival, and Art Deco.

Q. When it opened in 1899, Northern Arizona University had what name?

A. Northern Arizona Normal School.

Q. Who developed the first topographical map of the Grand Canyon region?

A. Francois Matthes.

Q. For whom was Moran Point named?

A. Thomas Moran, the landscape artist.

—ψ—

Q. Among the Hopi what are kachina dolls?

A. Representing spirits of the dead, they are carved wooden dolls used in religious ceremonies, particularly in pleas for a good harvest.

—ψ—

Q. What hotel on the Grand Canyon's South Rim architecturally resembles a European hunting lodge?

A. El Tovar.

—ψ—

Q. What was the name of Globe's early newspaper?

A. The *Silver Belt.*

—ψ—

Q. Who wrote *Ghost Towns of Arizona*?

A. James E. and Barbara H. Sherman.

—ψ—

Q. What U. S. Army officer who fought among the Apache Indians wrote the classic book about them entitled *Life Among the Apaches*?

A. John Carey Cremony.

—ψ—

Q. What Tucson museum features a large collection of sketches and models by Jacques Lipschitz?

A. The University of Arizona Museum of Art, located on campus.

Q. Who was the author of *The Last Chance: Tombstone's Early Years*?

A. John Myers.

—ψ—

Q. How many of Zane Grey's novels were set in Arizona?

A. Twenty-five.

—ψ—

Q. Dale L. Walker described the life and times of Buckey O'Neill in what book?

A. *Death Was the Black Horse.*

—ψ—

Q. James Ohio Pattie wrote what book when he returned East from his early adventures in present-day Arizona?

A. *The Personal Narrative of James O. Pattie.*

—ψ—

Q. Barry Goldwater collaborated with what author when he wrote his autobiography *Goldwater*?

A. Jack Casserly.

—ψ—

Q. What man who wrote *The Authentic Life of Billy, the Kid* was also the man who shot and killed him?

A. Pat Garrett.

—ψ—

Q. With three campuses, what is the oldest in Arizona's community college system?

A. Eastern Arizona College, at Thatcher, Gila Pueblo, and Payson.

Q. In 1859 who wrote in the *Weekly Arizonian,* "Conducting a newspaper in a frontier country is always a perilous, precarious and thankless task"?

A. The newspaper's editor, Edward E. Cross.

—ψ—

Q. Who is music director of the Tucson Symphony Orchestra?

A. George Hanson.

—ψ—

Q. What local newspaper described its town by writing, "[It] is a city set upon a hill, promising to vie with ancient Rome, upon her seven hills, in a fame different in character but no less in importance"?

A. The *Tombstone Epitaph.*

—ψ—

Q. Beginning publication in 1859, what was Arizona's first newspaper?

A. The *Weekly Arizonian,* Tubac.

—ψ—

Q. What was the reasoning for naming Tombstone's newspaper the *Tombstone Epitaph*?

A. According to its editor, "Every Tombstone needs an epitaph."

—ψ—

Q. Where was the first meeting of the Territorial Press Association of Arizona?

A. Phoenix, in 1890.

—ψ—

Q. Architect Mary Jane Colter designed what studio on the South Rim of the Grand Canyon to duplicate a Hopi Indian pueblo?

A. Lookout.

Q. Territorial governor and chancellor of the University of Arizona were two other positions held by what first president of the Territorial Press Association?

A. Louis C. Hughes.

—ᴪ—

Q. Who was the author of *Missions and Pueblos of the Old Southwest?*

A. Earle R. Forrest.

—ᴪ—

Q. What was historian Herbert Eugene Bolton's groundbreaking 1916 book?

A. *Spanish Explorations in the Southwest.*

—ᴪ—

Q. Who wrote an eight-volume study of Arizona history, the last of which was published in 1915?

A. Thomas Edwin Farish.

—ᴪ—

Q. *Apache Chronicle,* an outstanding study of the Apache people, was the work of what writer?

A. John Upton Terrell.

—ᴪ—

Q. What residential development in Prescott, futuristic in design, is the handiwork of Italian architect Paolo Soleri?

A. Arcosanti.

—ᴪ—

Q. What museum near Sierra Vista features military history in the Southwest, including a display of buffalo soldier items?

A. Fort Huachuca Museum.

Q. What Morenci artist is internationally known for his artwork depicting Native American and Southwest material?

A. Ted De Gracia.

—ψ—

Q. Where is De Gracia's Gallery in the Sun located?

A. Tucson.

—ψ—

Q. A dress-up room and a grocery store are two of the attractions at what Tucson museum?

A. The Tucson Children's Museum.

—ψ—

Q. A re-creation of a turn-of-the-century hotel is featured at what museum?

A. The Rim Country Museum in Payson.

—ψ—

Q. What is the highlight of the Scottsdale Museum of Contemporary Art?

A. The outdoor sculpture garden.

—ψ—

Q. What Tempe museum houses selections of art by Edward Hopper, Georgia O'Keeffe, and Norman Rockwell?

A. The Arizona State University Art Museum at the Nelson Fine Arts Center, on campus.

—ψ—

Q. What Clarksville, Tennessee, woman was noted for her scholarly writings about the Apache Indians?

A. Eve Ball.

Q. What architectural styles are reflected in Tempe's Niels Petersen House?

A. Queen Anne / Victorian.

—ψ—

Q. The building in Window Rock that houses the Navajo Nation Council Chambers resembles what Native American structure?

A. A Navajo hogan.

—ψ—

Q. Who wrote *Destiny Road: The Gila Trail and the Opening of the Southwest*?

A. Odie B. Faulk.

—ψ—

Q. What group was founded in 1981 in Phoenix by Daniel Hooper and now has an enrollment of two hundred girls, ages seven to eighteen?

A. Phoenix Girls Chorus, with Sue Kenly Marshall as artistic director.

—ψ—

Q. Why does the Jane Austen Society of North America, Southern Arizona Region, specify its dues are to be paid December 16?

A. It is Jane Austen's birthday.

—ψ—

Q. Arizona State University—West, in Phoenix, scheduled what big change in its curriculum for the fall semester 2001?

A. Adding lower division (freshman and sophomore) courses.

—ψ—

Q. *Jessie Benton Frémont*, a biography of the wife of territorial governor John C. Frémont, was written by what author?

A. Pamela Herr.

Q. The Fourteenth Annual Report of the Bureau of Ethnology, a U.S. government publication, contained in its 1896 issue a definitive account of what expedition?

A. Coronado.

—ψ—

Q. Who was the long-time editor of the revived *Tombstone Epitaph* and author of *The Tombstone Epitaph and John Philip Clum*?

A. Wallace E. Clayton.

—ψ—

Q. Who publishes *Arizona Highways*?

A. The Arizona Department of Transportation.

—ψ—

Q. What U.S. senator from Arizona masterminded the GI Bill that provided college educations for thousands of veterans of World War II?

A. Ernest W. McFarland.

—ψ—

Q. What Phoenix author wrote *The Curse of the Dutchman's Gold*?

A. Helen Corbin.

—ψ—

Q. In 1988 historian David Lavender wrote what book about the Colorado River?

A. *Colorado River Country.*

—ψ—

Q. What Tucson architect designed the building in which the Amerind Foundation in Willcox is housed?

A. H. M. Starkweather.

Q. In 1946 Frank Waters wrote what title for the Rivers of America series?

A. *The Colorado.*

Q. Two short story collections, *The Basket Woman* and *Lost Borders*, were written by what author who specialized in Native American culture and social problems?

A. Mary Austin.

Q. *Arizona: Historic Land,* published in 1982, was written by whom?

A. Bert Fireman.

Q. Nationally recognized authors autograph their books at the annual Brandeis Book and Author Luncheon in what city?

A. Scottsdale.

Q. What Arizona writer and historian wrote *Pioneer Heritage: The First Century of the Arizona Historical Society*?

A. C. L. "Doc" Sonnichsen.

Q. What late historian and college textbook writer lived in Sun City West?

A. Phillip H. Ault.

Q. What book best describes the life and times of the Arizona volunteers in the Spanish-American War?

A. *The Arizona Rough Riders,* by Charles Herner.

Q. What 1968 pamphlet by Bob Carr told the story of William H. Hardy and his 1865 skirmish with the Paiute Indians?

A. *A Night Ride in Arizona.*

—ψ—

Q. The Ansel Adams photographic archives are housed at what place?

A. The University of Arizona's Center for Creative Photography.

—ψ—

Q. What science bookstore is owned by an author and operated on the Internet?

A. Sci Fi—Arizona, Michael McCollum, proprietor.

—ψ—

Q. What group was formed for would-be women writers who have little time during the day to pursue their craft?

A. American Night Writers Association (formerly the Arizona Night Writers Association).

—ψ—

Q. The classic work, *The Snake Dance of the Hopi Indians*, was written by whom?

A. Earle R. Forrest.

—ψ—

Q. Which of the photographer Kolb brothers wrote *Through the Grand Canyon From Wyoming to Mexico*?

A. Ellsworth.

—ψ—

Q. In 1984 historian David Lavender published what booklet describing various episodes in Arizona history?

A. *Pipe Spring and the Arizona Strip.*

Q. Where does the Arizona Theater Company perform?

A. Herberger Theater in Phoenix.

Q. For what book did Zane Grey wish to be remembered?

A. *The Vanishing American*, which featured the plight of Native Americans.

Q. In what Phoenix facility does the Arizona Opera Company perform?

A. Phoenix Symphony Hall.

Q. What two writers coauthored *Tucson: The Life and Times of an American City*?

A. C. L. "Doc" Sonnichsen and Donald H. Bufkin.

Q. Godfrey Sykes wrote what book describing his adventures in Arizona?

A. *Westerly Trend.*

Q. In the 1850s John Udell kept what record, later published, of his family's tribulations in coming to the West?

A. *Journal of John Udell Kept During a Trip Across the Plains Containing an Account of the Massacre of a Portion of His Party by the Mohave Indians in 1858.*

Q. A field guide to southwestern cacti called *Cactus Country* was produced by what husband-wife team of Prescott?

A. Jim and Sue Willoughby.

Q. What is the largest high school in Arizona?

A. South Mountain, with thirty-four hundred students, grades nine through twelve.

_—ψ—_

Q. To whose adventures in Arizona and New Mexico did *Arizona Highways* devote its entire April 1984 issue?

A. Coronado.

_—ψ—_

Q. The Phoenix Public Library, with twelve branches, has how many holdings?

A. 1,797,247.

_—ψ—_

Q. *Vanished Arizona* was written by what author?

A. Martha Summerhayes.

_—ψ—_

Q. What prolific novelist of the 1920s through the 1950s later became a historian and wrote *Apache Crossing*?

A. Harry Sinclair Drago.

_—ψ—_

Q. Who wrote the recent biography *Nellie Cashman: Frontier Angel*?

A. Ron W. Fischer.

_—ψ—_

Q. Who wrote *The Big Rock Candy Mountain,* a Pulitzer Prize and National Book Award winner, which tells the story of an American family moving from place to place in the West?

A. Wallace Stegner.

Q. Oliver H. La Farge received what award in 1929 for his novel *Laughing Boy* about the Navajo Indians?

A. Pulitzer Prize.

Q. Who are the central characters in many of Tony Hillerman's novels about Navajoland?

A. Joe Leaphorn and Jim Chee.

Q. Tony Hillerman's fictional characters Joe Leaphorn and Jim Chee pursue what profession?

A. They are members of the Navajo Tribal Police force.

Q. What Arizona rancher's life was depicted in the 1889 Broadway play *Arizona: A Drama in Four Acts*?

A. Henry Clay Hooker.

Q. What member of the Chiricahua Apache tribe was a book illustrator and an artist of international note?

A. Allan Houser.

Q. Who wrote *Brothers Five: The Babbitts of Arizona*?

A. Dean Smith.

Q. What former U.S. army officer and one-time aide-de-camp to Gen. George Crook produced ten authoritative ethnological books about the customs, history, and lifestyles of southwestern Indians?

A. John Gregory Bourke.

Q. What was perhaps Bourke's most popular book?

A. *On the Border with Crook,* published in 1891.

Q. *The Martian Chronicles, Fahrenheit 451,* and the first episode of *Twilight Zone* were written by what imaginative Arizona resident?

A. Ray Bradbury.

Q. Who wrote the book *The Death of Warren Baxter Earp,* in observance of the one hundredth anniversary of Earp's death in Willcox?

A. Michael M. Hickey.

Q. What Arizona resident authored the monumental, four-volume *Encyclopedia of Frontier Biography*?

A. Dan L. Thrapp.

Q. What Phoenix newspaperman is also a best-selling author of western novels?

A. John Legg, whose novels include *Guns of Apache Springs* and *Arizona Coffin.*

Q. What Scottsdale personal trainer is also the author of cookbooks such as *The Fat-Free Living Family Cookbook*?

A. Jyl Steinback.

Q. Who wrote the 1932 book *Pioneer Days in Arizona*?

A. Frank C. Lockwood.

Q. What Tucson museum preserves material objects, including the most comprehensive collection of Hohokam artifacts in existence, and interprets the history of southwestern cultures?

A. Arizona State Museum.

–ψ–

Q. The popular book *Helldorado* was written by whom?

A. William M. Breckenridge.

–ψ–

Q. In 1997 what native of Prescott was awarded the *Arizona Game and Fish* magazine Outdoor Writer of the Year Award?

A. Ronald Harris.

–ψ–

Q. Who is music director for the Phoenix Symphony Orchestra?

A. Hermann Michael.

–ψ–

Q. Drawn primarily from Yuma and La Paz Counties, seven thousand students attend what junior college located five miles east of Yuma?

A. Arizona Western College.

–ψ–

Q. What two magazines of western history recently relocated their offices from Oklahoma to Cave Creek?

A. *True West* and *Old West Journal.*

–ψ–

Q. In what city is the magazine *Native People* published?

A. Phoenix.

Q. What book published by the University of Arizona Press features the outstanding photographs of John Annerino?

A. *Canyons of the Southwest.*

—ψ—

Q. Who is the author of *Apache Voices*, which is based on the papers of the late Arizona writer Eve Ball?

A. Sherry Robinson.

—ψ—

Q. What biography of Grand Canyon explorer John Wesley Powell won a Spur Award in 2001 from Western Writers of America?

A. *A River Running West,* by Donald Worster.

—ψ—

Q. Tucson author Jane Eppinga compiled what photographic collection about the history of her hometown?

A. *Images of America: Tucson, Arizona.*

—ψ—

Q. The Madonna of the Trail monument to pioneer women may be seen in what town?

A. Springerville.

—ψ—

Q. What Zane Grey novel had as its setting the Graham-Tewksbury feud?

A. *To the Last Man.*

—ψ—

Q. Who wrote *Ambush at Bloody Run*, the true story of the 1889 Wham Paymaster robbery near Pima?

A. Larry D. Ball.

Q. Who wrote the definitive *History of Arizona and New Mexico*?

A. Hubert Howe Bancroft.

—ψ—

Q. *The Conquest of Apacheria* and *Al Sieber, Chief of Scouts*, both dealing with Arizona subjects, were written by what author?

A. Dan Thrapp.

—ψ—

Q. In just eleven weeks what prolific former newspaper reporter wrote the historical novel *Apache* about Mangas Coloradas?

A. Will Levington Comfort.

—ψ—

Q. Three times each school year, the Music Educators Association puts out what publication?

A. *Arizona Music News*, established 1939.

—ψ—

Q. South Mountain High School is made up of four magnet schools in what fields?

A. Law, aerospace, communications, and art.

—ψ—

Q. What group that meets bimonthly in Camp Verde is dedicated to improving the writing and professional knowledge of both published and unpublished authors in a particular field?

A. Northern Arizona Romance Writers of America (NARWA).

—ψ—

Q. What percentage of the circulation of *Arizona Highways* magazine is out of state?

A. 80 percent.

Q. What writer of fiction and historical nonfiction said that he tried to express in his work "the geography of promise" that the West symbolizes?

A. Wallace Stegner.

_ψ_

Q. Fine Art Weekend, when artists open their studios, share techniques, and give demonstrations, takes place each March in what town?

A. Oracle.

_ψ_

Q. As part of the continuing Wyatt Earp mania, what two books were published in 1998 and 1999 about the hero of the gunfight at the O. K. Corral?

A. *Inventing Wyatt Earp* (1998), by Allen Barra, and *Wyatt Earp, Life Behind the Legend* (1999), by Casey Tefertiller.

_ψ_

Q. What Willcox resident, who is also a noted horsewoman, is the author of *Nine Days at Dragoon Springs* and appears regularly at the Warren Earp Days in Willcox?

A. Phyllis Morreale-de la Garza.

_ψ_

Q. Grace Cooke wrote what romantic novel in 1913 about life on the Hopi Indian Reservation?

A. *The Joy Bringer: A Tale of the Painted Desert.*

_ψ_

Q. Paul Horgan, the 1954 Pulitzer Prize winner for his two-volume history of the Rio Grande, wrote what book describing nineteenth-century military life in the Southwest?

A. *A Distant Trumpet.*

Q. What husband and wife—he professor emeritus of English at the University of Arizona and she the former director of the UA Poetry Center—have written extensively about their state?

A. Dr. L. D. and LaVerne Harrell Clark.

—ψ—

Q. At Rawhide, a re-creation of an 1880s western town near Scottsdale, what four-day event includes a western film festival, a cowboy trade show, and cowboy poetry reading?

A. Festival of the West.

SPORTS & LEISURE

Q. What Arizona female softball pitcher was memorialized in the film *A League of Their Own*?

A. Charlotte "Skipper" Armstrong.

Q. In 1945 Skipper Armstrong accomplished what feat while playing with the South Bend Blue Sox?

A. She pitched shutouts in both games (a total of thirty-two innings) of a double-header.

Q. Where was Superbowl XXX played?

A. At Arizona State University's Sun Devil Stadium in Tempe.

Q. What record did Superbowl XXX in 1996, between the Pittsburgh Steelers and the Dallas Cowboys, break?

A. It had more viewers that any TV program to date.

Q. Tourists on the Navajo Reservation should ask permission of the residents of this sovereign nation before pursuing what quite common activity?

A. Photographing the people, their homes, or their possessions.

Q. At what dam may tourists put on hard hats and tour the inner workings of the dam?

A. Hoover.

Q. On what NFL team did Arizona State great Cecil Mulleneaux play from 1932 till 1941?

A. New York Giants.

Q. New residents must reside in Arizona for how long before they can purchase a hunting license?

A. Six months.

Q. Where does the Milwaukee Brewers baseball club conduct its spring training?

A. Maryvale Baseball Park in Phoenix.

Q. What former New York Yankees manager also managed the Arizona Diamondbacks during their early years?

A. "Buck" Showalter.

Q. Who won Superbowl XXX?

A. Dallas with a score of 27–17.

Q. The 1983 Indianapolis 500 automobile race was won by what Arizonan?

A. Tom Sneva.

Q. Who won the 1934 Phoenix Open golf championship?

A. Barry Goldwater.

—ψ—

Q. In what year did the Phoenix Suns begin play in Arizona?

A. 1968.

—ψ—

Q. The only person to win both the Academy Award and the Professional World Cowboy championship was what Arizonan?

A. Ben Johnson.

—ψ—

Q. A major league baseball team first conducted its spring training in Arizona in what year?

A. 1947.

—ψ—

Q. What major league baseball team was first to hold its spring training in Arizona?

A. The Cleveland Indians.

—ψ—

Q. Where in Phoenix is the venue for dragboat racing?

A. Firebird Raceway.

—ψ—

Q. What well-known coach for the New York Yankees played his first professional baseball with the old Class C Phoenix Senators?

A. Billy Martin.

Q. Shawn Collins has what "first" in his record?

A. First Northern Arizona University football player to become a first round draft pick in the NFL.

—ψ—

Q. How many year-round fishing locations does the state have?

A. Around five hundred.

—ψ—

Q. Who played baseball for the Globe-Miami Browns and went on to pitch a perfect game for the New York Yankees in the 1955 World Series?

A. Don Larsen.

—ψ—

Q. What golfer won three consecutive Phoenix Opens?

A. Arnold Palmer.

—ψ—

Q. The winner of the 1958 Indianapolis 500 was what Arizonan?

A. Jimmy Bryan.

—ψ—

Q. Both prominent in national politics, what two brothers played basketball at the University of Arizona?

A. Stewart and Morris Udall.

—ψ—

Q. The Cy Young–winning pitcher Jim Palmer attended what school in Scottsdale?

A. Scottsdale High School.

Q. Who was the first coach of the Phoenix Cardinals?

A. Gene Stallings.

—ψ—

Q. At the Atlanta Olympics in 1996, what Arizonan spearheaded the American women's gymnastics team to a gold medal victory?

A. Kerri Strug.

—ψ—

Q. Who was the first black pitcher to hurl a victory in the World Series?

A. Joe Black, pitching for the 1952 Brooklyn Dodgers team.

—ψ—

Q. At the first NFL Superbowl in Los Angeles in 1967, what band played the national anthem?

A. University of Arizona.

—ψ—

Q. A new program at the State Fair allows children to earn a free ride by doing what?

A. Reading books.

—ψ—

Q. What Arizona football team won the 1987 Rose Bowl?

A. Arizona State University.

—ψ—

Q. What Arizonan was named 1993 Fighter of the Year by *Ring* magazine?

A. Michael Carbajal.

Q. For one to make a muleback trip into the Grand Canyon, what are the four physical requirements?

A. Be over four feet, seven inches tall; weigh less than two hundred pounds (including clothes and equipment); not be pregnant; be in good physical condition.

Q. What amazing feat did baseball player Bob Horner accomplish when he played for the Atlanta Braves?

A. Hitting four home runs in one game.

Q. To which league does the Phoenix Mercury Club belong?

A. The WNBA (Women's National Basketball Association).

Q. What is the name of Tempe's baseball stadium?

A. Diablo.

Q. The Colorado Rockies train in what Arizona city?

A. Tucson.

—ψ—

Q. The Navajo Nation Annual Tribal Fair at Window Rock has what special distinction?

A. It is the nation's largest Native American fair.

—ψ—

Q. How many golf courses are in Arizona?

A. Approximately 275.

Q. Exchanging blows with Muhammad Ali in 1967 for the world heavyweight championship was what boxer from Chandler?

A. Zora Folley.

—ψ—

Q. Since joining the tour in 1998, what Scottsdale golfer has had two Senior PGA victories?

A. Gary McCord.

—ψ—

Q. Where do the Andy Devine Days and the PRCA Rodeo take place?

A. Kingman.

—ψ—

Q. What is the University of Arizona's nickname?

A. Wildcats.

—ψ—

Q. In what sport did the University of Arizona first excel?

A. Polo.

—ψ—

Q. Where did the Arizona Cardinals play before they moved to Phoenix in 1988?

A. St. Louis.

—ψ—

Q. Where did the Cardinals play before they moved to St. Louis?

A. Chicago.

Q. Before March 1994 the Arizona Cardinals were known by what name?

A. Phoenix Cardinals.

—ψ—

Q. What significant record does the Arizona Cardinals team hold in the NFL?

A. Oldest continuous franchise in the league.

—ψ—

Q. Where in Tempe can children and families play in the snow in July?

A. At the annual Downtown Cooldown.

—ψ—

Q. The largest fishing clinic in the state, held at Clear Creek Recreation Area, is sponsored by what group?

A. Winslow Jaycees.

—ψ—

Q. Which Arizona college was one of the first in the nation to accept, as far back as the 1930s, black athletes into its sports programs?

A. Arizona State University.

—ψ—

Q. Who were the original four owners of the Phoenix Suns?

A. Andy Williams, Ed Ames, Bobbie Gentry, and Henry Mancini.

—ψ—

Q. Where was the nation's first organized rodeo held?

A. Prescott, on July 4, 1888.

Q. Where does the Chicago White Sox baseball club conduct its spring training?

A. Tucson Electric Park in Tucson.

Q. What was one of the earliest sports played in Tombstone?

A. Baseball.

Q. Arizona has what two national recreational areas?

A. Glen Canyon and Lake Mead.

Q. What is the name of the group of major league baseball teams who use locales in Arizona as sites for spring training?

A. The Cactus League.

Q. Winner of five U.S. amateur golf championships, what Arizona State alumnus was inducted into the LPGA Hall of Fame in 1982?

A. JoAnn Gunderson Carner.

Q. What common identity did teams such as the Lettuce Kings, Funk Jewelers, A1 Queens, and PBSW Ramblers have?

A. They were all teams in the old Phoenix fast-pitch softball leagues.

Q. Who was the "greatest woman athlete in Arizona history," according to many sources?

A. Dot Wilkinson.

Q. Where was the old Phoenix Softball Park located?

A. At 15th Avenue and Roosevelt.

—ψ—

Q. How does Arizona rank in the nation with respect to number of state parks?

A. Fortieth.

—ψ—

Q. Where did Phoenix Open champ Phil Mickelson attend college?

A. Arizona State University.

—ψ—

Q. Snowflake holds what annual July event that features a parade, barbecue, rodeo, softball league tournament, and fireworks?

A. Pioneer Day Celebration.

—ψ—

Q. To what league does the women's basketball team the Phoenix Mercury belong?

A. The Women's National Basketball Association.

—ψ—

Q. In what city did the Phoenix Coyotes hockey team formerly play?

A. Winnipeg.

—ψ—

Q. Freshmen at the University of Arizona annually do what to Sentinel Peak in a Tucson park?

A. Whitewash a big *A* on it, thus giving it its popular name of "A Mountain."

Q. What professional team plays at Cataline High School throughout the summer?

A. Tucson Fireballs soccer team.

—ψ—

Q. The Mexican government charges what fee for tourists to cross the border into Mexico for business or pleasure?

A. 150 pesos (approximately $15 U.S.).

—ψ—

Q. What three national parks are in Arizona?

A. Grand Canyon, Petrified Forest, and Saguaro National Parks.

—ψ—

Q. In 1991, 1993, and 1994 who led the UofA's women's softball team to NCAA championships?

A. Susie Parra.

—ψ—

Q. Spring training for the Anaheim Angels takes place in what stadium?

A. Tempe Diablo.

—ψ—

Q. Where do the Arizona Diamondbacks conduct spring training?

A. Tucson.

—ψ—

Q. Former miners conduct tours by mine car into what underground mine?

A. Queen.

Q. When did major league baseball come to Arizona?

A. 1998, with the first game of the Arizona Diamondbacks, although the team's franchise was awarded in 1995.

Q. What Arizonan from Wickenburg won the 1992 PRCA bull-riding championship?

A. Cody Custer.

Q. A native Arizonan, what woman tennis great won the U.S. singles championship four consecutive years, 1932 through 1935, and Wimbledon in 1936?

A. Helen Hull Jacobs.

Q. What city on the Nevada border is noted for its water sports?

A. Bullhead City.

Q. Who was ASU's first four-time All-American in golf?

A. Billy Mayfair.

Q. In what city do the Chicago Cubs conduct spring training?

A. Mesa.

Q. In 1993 the NBA's MVP was what Phoenix Suns player?

A. Charles Barkley.

Q. On May 5 many Arizona communities celebrate Cinco de Mayo, a Mexican holiday honoring what event?

A. Victory of the Mexican army over an invading French force at Puebla in 1862.

—ψ—

Q. In what league and division do the Arizona Diamondbacks play?

A. National League, Western Division.

—ψ—

Q. Where do the Arizona Diamondbacks play regular season baseball?

A. Bank One Ballpark in downtown Phoenix.

—ψ—

Q. Bank One Ballpark is called by what name informally?

A. BOB.

—ψ—

Q. Where do the Arizona Cardinals play football?

A. Tempe.

—ψ—

Q. No photographing, painting, recording, or sketching is permitted at what Native American reservation?

A. Hopi.

—ψ—

Q. Ostrich racing takes place each March at what event?

A. Chandler Ostrich Festival.

Q. What is the seating capacity of the America West Arena?

A. Twenty thousand.

—ψ—

Q. The America West Arena was built as a cooperative effort between what two parties?

A. America West Airlines and the Phoenix Suns owner Michael Colangelo.

—ψ—

Q. The America West Arena was built to be home to what sports team?

A. The Phoenix Suns.

—ψ—

Q. In Kayenta, Fourth of July celebrations feature what activities?

A. Fireworks, a rodeo, and dancing.

—ψ—

Q. How many fans did the Phoenix Mercury draw in the year 2000?

A. Four hundred thousand.

—ψ—

Q. What former spring training site for the San Francisco Giants has a swimming pool shaped like a baseball bat?

A. Francisco Grande Resort and Golf Club at Casa Grande.

—ψ—

Q. The San Francisco Giants go to what city for spring training?

A. Scottsdale.

Q. What town claims to host the world's oldest continuous rodeo?

A. Payson.

—ψ—

Q. What minor league hockey team belongs to Tucson?

A. The Tucson Scorch.

—ψ—

Q. Known for his golf commentaries and broadcasts is what Paradise Valley resident?

A. Peter Kostis.

—ψ—

Q. Who are the Tucson Sidewinders?

A. The AAA minor league baseball team in Tucson.

—ψ—

Q. With which major league baseball team are the Tucson Sidewinders affiliated?

A. The Arizona Diamondbacks.

—ψ—

Q. For what softball team did former Arizona governor Rose Mofford once play?

A. The A1 Queens.

—ψ—

Q. In what track event did ASU's Mike Barrick, Henry Carr, Ron Freeman, and Ulis Williams set a world record in 1963?

A. The one-mile relay.

Q. "Cactus Comet" was the nickname of what University of Arizona football player?

A. J. F. "Pop" McKale.

—ψ—

Q. What Phoenix resident invented the Ping golf club?

A. Karsten Solheim.

—ψ—

Q. Where is the Western Navajo Fair held annually?

A. Tuba City.

—ψ—

Q. Who was named College Football Coach of the Year in 1975?

A. Frank Kush of Arizona State.

—ψ—

Q. In the 2000 National Outdoor Rifle and Pistol championship, what Prescott woman won for high power rifle long range?

A. Michelle M. Gallagher.

—ψ—

Q. In 1950 what college football player led the nation in yards rushing?

A. Whizzer White.

—ψ—

Q. What major league baseball player originally attended ASU to play football?

A. Reggie Jackson.

Q. The great rivalry between the UofA and ASU football teams began in what year?

A. 1899.

—ᴪ—

Q. At what community is the start for most raft trips down the Colorado River?

A. Lee's Ferry.

—ᴪ—

Q. Former Dallas Cowboy Danny White attended what high school?

A. Westwood.

—ᴪ—

Q. Who leads the Arizona Rattlers?

A. Former Dallas Cowboy quarterback Danny White.

—ᴪ—

Q. In what two years did the Arizona Rattlers win the Arena Football League championship?

A. 1994 and 1997.

—ᴪ—

Q. Where do the Arizona Rattlers play?

A. America West Arena in Phoenix.

—ᴪ—

Q. Against whom did the ASU basketball team play its first game?

A. Mesa High School

Q. What is the UofA's marching band called?

A. The Pride of Arizona.

Q. The first Arizonan to win a world boxing championship was what Globe native?

A. Louis Espinoza.

Q. Who won the Fiesta Bowl in 1994?

A. UofA Wildcats.

Q. Who was the Phoenix Suns' first coach?

A. Johnny "Red" Kerr.

Q. What were Arizona's two professional football teams before the Cardinals?

A. The Arizona Wranglers and the Arizona Outlaws.

Q. The Sunrise Ski Area is owned and operated by what Native Americans?

A. The White Mountain Apache.

Q. Who is the only ASU baseball player ever to pitch a perfect game?

A. Eddie Bane.

Q. What annual October event in Willcox honors the town's favorite son?

A. Rex Allen Days.

—ψ—

Q. What is Phoenix's AAA baseball team?

A. The Phoenix Firebirds.

—ψ—

Q. What Phoenix eye surgeon medaled for swimming in the 1968, 1972, and 1976 Olympics?

A. Gary Hall Sr.

—ψ—

Q. Who led the men's gold-medal-winning swimming team in the 1996 Olympics?

A. Gary Hall Jr.

—ψ—

Q. At what golf facility is the Phoenix Open played?

A. Scottsdale TPC Course.

—ψ—

Q. When was the first Copper Bowl played?

A. 1989, in Tucson's Arizona Stadium.

—ψ—

Q. Who is the only fast-pitch softball player to win All-American honors in three playing positions—pitcher, out-field, and first base?

A. Margie Law.

Q. For whom is the McKale Memorial Center on the University of Arizona's campus named?

A. J. F. "Pop" McKale, a former football coach and athletic director.

—ψ—

Q. The Seattle Mariners and the Oakland A's have spring training in what Arizona town?

A. Peoria.

—ψ—

Q. The first person to be inducted into the American Cowgirl Hall of Fame was what Tucson woman?

A. Alice Greenaugh.

—ψ—

Q. In 1947 who brought major league baseball to Arizona?

A. Bill Veeck, when he brought his Cleveland Indians to Tucson to train.

—ψ—

Q. Geronimo and his Apache raiders are said to have interrupted what kind of sporting event?

A. A baseball game.

—ψ—

Q. Legendary in Arizona sports is what husband-wife fast-pitch softball pitching team?

A. Margie and Kenny Law.

—ψ—

Q. What is the name of ASU's mascot?

A. Sparky.

Q. Winning the 1996 Phoenix Open was what ASU golf star?

A. Phil Mickelson.

Q. Later a television personality, what young lady was the 1978 Fiesta Bowl queen?

A. Jineane Ford.

Q. Hall of Famer Willie McCovey once played for what Arizona baseball team?

A. The Phoenix Giants of the AAA Pacific Coast League.

Q. Why is the summit of Mount Baldy near Greer off-limits to non-Apaches?

A. It is on the White Mountain Apache Indian Reservation.

Q. The Northern Arizona University football team belongs to what conference?

A. Big Sky.

Q. In 1982 what Casa Grande resident became the first black PRCA bull-riding champion?

A. Charlie Sampson.

Q. Formerly a ball player at Grand Canyon University, who was named American League Rookie of the Year in 1993?

A. Tim Salmon.

Q. What Scottsdale resident is noted for his golf instruction schools?

A. John Jacobs.

Q. Grand Canyon University's mascot is what animal?

A. Antelope.

Q. In 1947 what baseball Hall of Famer pitched the first game played in the Cactus League?

A. Bob Lemon.

Q. In the early days of their spring training in Arizona, the Cleveland Indian players stayed in what Tucson hotel?

A. Santa Rita.

Q. In addition to being the "Voice of the Phoenix Suns," what other interest does broadcaster Al McCoy have?

A. He is an accomplished jazz pianist.

Q. What animal is the Phoenix Suns' mascot?

A. Gorilla.

Q. Where are the Goodyear Rodeo Days held?

A. At the Estrella Mountain Regional Park.

Q. A charter member of the Arizona Sports Hall of Fame, what UofA's baseball coach has a ballpark named for him?

A. Frank Sancet.

—ψ—

Q. As an Arizona resident what legendary baseball player became a broadcast commentator?

A. Joe Garagiola.

—ψ—

Q. What LPGA favorite from Arizona was honored with a special award in 1994?

A. Heather Farr.

—ψ—

Q. What National League Most Valuable Player played baseball at ASU?

A. Barry Bonds.

—ψ—

Q. Where is the Rodeo of Rodeos held?

A. Phoenix.

—ψ—

Q. In 1950 what was the first Arizona sports event televised?

A. The Salad Bowl.

—ψ—

Q. What is the nickname for Northern Arizona University sports teams?

A. The Lumberjacks.

Q. What soon-to-be outstanding basketball player did the Phoenix Suns lose to the Milwaukee Bucks in a 1969 coin flip?

A. Lew Alcindor, later known as Kareem Abdul-Jabbar.

Q. What Mesa resident participated in both the 1960 and 1964 Olympics, winning a bronze medal in the 1964 three-meter competition?

A. Patsy Willard.

Q. Who were the first two Arizonans to play professional football?

A. Carl "Moose" Mulleneaux and his brother Cecil.

Q. What is the world's largest horse-drawn parade called?

A. Parada del Sol, in Scottsdale.

Q. Barry Bonds and Reggie Jackson both wore what jersey number during their careers at Arizona State University?

A. 24.

Q. What UofA basketball player was the first to have his jersey retired?

A. Sean Elliott.

Q. For riding a wild buffalo at a Prescott rodeo in 1904, what Arizonan became known as "the man who rode the buffalo"?

A. John Francis "Frank" Condron.

Q. Who was the first Arizona Diamondback player to score both a regular season hit and a regular season home run?

A. Travis Lee, on March 31, 1998.

—Ψ—

Q. What Arizona-related record does the great baseball player Willie Mays hold?

A. He hit the first home run out of Phoenix Municipal Stadium (1964).

—Ψ—

Q. The 1955 Kentucky Derby winner, "Swaps," was owned by what member of a longtime Arizona family?

A. Rex Ellsworth.

—Ψ—

Q. Born in Phoenix, now a Scottsdale resident, who recently joined the ranks of senior pro golfers?

A. Howard Twitty.

—Ψ—

Q. What University of Arizona basketball player walked away with the 1990 Player of the Year award?

A. Sean Elliott.

—Ψ—

Q. What national championship did the University of Arizona Wildcats win in 1997?

A. The NCAA basketball championship.

—Ψ—

Q. What three sports did the legendary coach Bill Kajikawa play at Arizona State University?

A. Baseball, football, and basketball.

Q. Winning the PRCA All-around Cowboy award every year from 1989 to 1994 was what Phoenix rodeo star?

A. Ty Murray.

—ψ—

Q. Who were two former governors of Arizona who were also associated with the Arizona State University sports programs?

A. Ben Moeur and Jack Williams.

—ψ—

Q. The oldest such accommodation in America, the livery stable at the Grand Canyon opened for business in what year?

A. 1902.

—ψ—

Q. Where does the Phoenix Mercury club play?

A. America West Arena.

—ψ—

Q. What Arizonan first attained a speed of 200 mph at the Indianapolis 500?

A. Tom Sneva.

—ψ—

Q. The ASU Sun Devils originally had what nickname?

A. Bulldogs.

—ψ—

Q. What National Cutting Horse Association champion and 1962 inductee into the National Cowboy Hall of Fame once owned ranches in Arizona?

A. Edward Bowman.

Q. Dot Wilkinson, described by some as the best woman athlete in Arizona history, excelled at what two sports?

A. Fast-pitch softball and bowling.

—ψ—

Q. Who was the first Arizona coach to become a member of the College Football Hall of Fame?

A. Dan Devine.

—ψ—

Q. How many golf courses does the greater Phoenix area boast?

A. Around one hundred.

—ψ—

Q. *USA Today* named what annual event in Tempe one of America's top eight places to spend New Year's Eve?

A. The Fiesta Bowl Block Party.

—ψ—

Q. What former UofA football player won the NCAA long jump championship and later played for the Denver Broncos?

A. Vance Johnson.

—ψ—

Q. What Gilbert native was half of the PRCA team that won five consecutive PRCA-sponsored team roping events from 1985 to 1989, and again in 1992 and 1994?

A. Clay O'Brian Cooper.

—ψ—

Q. What is the largest outdoor midwinter rodeo in America?

A. Tucson's La Fiesta de los Vaqueros.

Q. At what two courses is the Touchstone Energy Tucson Open golf tournament held?

A. Starr Pass and Tucson National.

—ψ—

Q. When is the Gila County Fair held?

A. September.

—ψ—

Q. What lake near Greer is a haven for fishermen in search of rainbow and brown trout?

A. Bunch Reservoir.

—ψ—

Q. What Ahwatukee resident won the 2001 Phoenix Open golf tournament?

A. Mark Calcavecchia.

—ψ—

Q. Who coached women's tennis at Arizona State University for thirty years and is a member of ASU's Hall of Distinction?

A. Anne Pittman.

—ψ—

Q. The Phoenix Coyotes use what facility to play?

A. America West Arena.

—ψ—

Q. What star running back at Mesa High School and ASU later played for the Chicago Bears?

A. Wilford "Whizzer" White.

SCIENCE & NATURE

C H A P T E R   S I X

Q. Underlying the soil in some parts of Arizona's lowlands is lime rock, called by what technical name, which may be so hard that power tools are needed to dig holes?

A. Caliche.

Q. Arizona boasts that it has how many days of sunshine throughout the year?

A. Over three hundred.

Q. To explore the meandering trails of the Grand Canyon, what animal is primarily used?

A. The mule.

Q. Although crops are grown on only about 5 percent of the farmland, they account for about half of Arizona's farm income, with what other products accounting for the other half?

A. Livestock and livestock products.

Q. What did Lowell call the planet that he predicted would someday be discovered orbiting the sun, a feat which was accomplished later at Lowell Observatory?

A. Planet X.

Q. Of the two thousand species of cacti, how many are native to the Southwest?

A. About one hundred.

—ψ—

Q. In 1929 what astronomer at the University of Arizona developed the new science of dendrochronology, or dating past events by studying successive tree rings?

A. Andrew Ellicott Douglass.

—ψ—

Q. In 1973 Andrew Ellicott Douglass established what scientific center at the University of Arizona?

A. The Laboratory of Tree-Ring Research.

—ψ—

Q. The ninth planet, Pluto, was discovered in 1930 by what astronomy assistant at the Lowell Observatory in Flagstaff?

A. Clyde W. Tombaugh.

—ψ—

Q. When was Lowell Observatory in Flagstaff established?

A. 1894.

—ψ—

Q. For whom was Lowell Observatory named?

A. Percival Lowell.

—ψ—

Q. Cacti are members of what large plant family?

A. Succulents.

Q. What is the estimated age of the Grand Canyon?

A. Two billion years.

—ψ—

Q. What cactus that can weigh ten tons and reach a height of sixty feet grows only in parts of Arizona, California, and Mexico?

A. The saguaro.

—ψ—

Q. A nonmotorized hiking path, the Arizona Trail is how many miles long?

A. 750.

—ψ—

Q. What is the state tree of Arizona?

A. The paloverde or green-barked acacia.

—ψ—

Q. What Arizona city is known as "the astronomy capital of the world"?

A. Tucson.

—ψ—

Q. How many observatories are situated in the Tucson area?

A. Thirty.

—ψ—

Q. What chain of convenience stores that also provides gasoline service has its corporate headquarters in Phoenix?

A. Circle K.

Q. What is the state bird of Arizona?

A. The cactus wren.

—ψ—

Q. What major U.S. transportation company is based in Phoenix?

A. America West Airlines.

—ψ—

Q. How many national forests are located in Arizona?

A. Seven.

—ψ—

Q. The Colorado river runs how many miles within Arizona's boundaries?

A. 688.

—ψ—

Q. What species of mammal is confined to the southwestern half of Arizona and part of northern Mexico?

A. Yuma antelope squirrel.

—ψ—

Q. Which variety of cactus traditionally leans toward the south, thus causing it to be called the "compass cactus"?

A. The Arizona barrel cactus.

—ψ—

Q. How high is Hoover Dam?

A. 726.4 feet, about the length of two football fields, from goalpost to goalpost, placed end to end.

Q. In 1999 the estimated amount of timber-lumber production (pine, fir, and spruce) in Arizona was how many board feet?

A. 98 million.

—ψ—

Q. What species of squirrel lives on both the North and the South Rims of the Grand Canyon, the northern variety being considered by some scientists to be a distinct species?

A. Tassel-eared squirrel.

—ψ—

Q. The last grizzly bear killed in Arizona was in what year?

A. 1935.

—ψ—

Q. How many nursing homes are registered in the state?

A. 163.

—ψ—

Q. Why are there no fish in Montezuma Well, the large sinkhole that was the water source for the ancient peoples?

A. The calcium content from the underlying limestone is too high to support much underwater life.

—ψ—

Q. Begun in 1925 to train airplane pilots, what coed institution has two residential campuses, in Daytona Beach, Florida, and Prescott, Arizona, and 129 teaching centers in the United States and Europe?

A. Embry-Riddle Aeronautical University.

—ψ—

Q. As of January 2000, how many cattle/calves were in Arizona?

A. 840,000.

Q. During World War II why were many air bases established in Arizona?

A. The large number of sunny days provided ideal flying weather.

—ψ—

Q. In October 2000 what company announced plans to build a $540 million, 1,080-megawatt natural gas–fired merchant generating facility in La Paz County to be completed in 2005?

A. Allegheny Energy Supply Company.

—ψ—

Q. What is the teen birthrate per one thousand for females aged seventeen to nineteen?

A. 70.5, compared to 51 national average (1998 figures).

—ψ—

Q. Which species of cacti is found only in Santa Cruz County and part of neighboring Sonora, Mexico?

A. Golden pincushion

—ψ—

Q. What is a butte?

A. A hill that rises abruptly from a surrounding area, with sloping sides and a flat top.

—ψ—

Q. What endangered species of bird ranges in Arizona, California, and Baja California?

A. California condor.

—ψ—

Q. How many hazardous waste sites are in the state?

A. Seventeen, three federal facilities and fourteen general superfund sites.

Q. In the metropolitan Phoenix-Mesa area how many days failed to meet acceptable air quality standards in 1999?

A. Twelve, down from seventeen in 1998.

Q. In one of the most desertic places in the United States, near Gold Spring on Navajo and Hopi Reservation land, what governmental project collected geometeorological data from 1979 to 1992?

A. The U.S. Geological Survey Desert Winds Project.

Q. In the period 1977–1999, how many executions took place in the state?

A. Nineteen, seventeen by lethal injection and two by lethal gas.

Q. The average wind speed in Phoenix is how many miles per hour?

A. 6.2, with the highest recorded at 43.

Q. In 1999 what was the average acreage per farm?

A. 3,571.

Q. Meteor Crater, designated a natural landmark, is owned by the family of what man who in 1903 filed a claim to mine the crater for iron?

A. Daniel Moreau Barringer.

Q. Of the six "forests" in the Petrified Forest National Park, which is the most colorful?

A. Rainbow, the others being First, Second, Third, Black, and Blue.

Q. What iron oxide minerals create bright red and bright yellow in the Painted Desert?

A. Hematite (red) and limonite (yellow).

Q. What percentage of Arizona's land area is defined as true desert?

A. Less than one percent.

Q. The best-known waterfalls—Beaver, Bridal Veil, Havasu, Mooney, and Navajo—are all on what creek in the Supai Canyon area of the Grand Canyon?

A. Havasu.

Q. How many kinds of lizards, including the poisonous Gila monster, inhabit Arizona?

A. Around forty.

Q. What dry stream runs through the Buenos Aires National Wildlife Refuge?

A. Brawley Wash.

Q. In 1985 what percentage of the nation's copper did Arizona produce?

A. 72 percent.

Q. The Central Arizona Project, designed to eventually transport nearly three million acre-feet of water from the Colorado River to regional urban centers, was dedicated in what year?

A. 1985.

Q. What member of the raccoon family lives in the southeastern quadrant of Arizona?

A. Coati.

—ψ—

Q. Besides Arizona, what seven other states have uranium reserves?

A. Colorado, Nebraska, New Mexico, Texas, Utah, Washington, and Wyoming.

—ψ—

Q. How high is the BankOne Center In Phoenix?

A. 480 feet and 40 stories.

—ψ—

Q. What well-known Arizona family recently donated a thirty-five-thousand-acre easement on the South Rim of the Grand Canyon to the Nature Conservancy?

A. Babbitt.

—ψ—

Q. Where is the world's largest solar telescope located?

A. Kitt Peak National Observatory, seventy miles southwest of Tucson.

—ψ—

Q. Where is the full range of Arizona's gem and mineral wealth displayed in Phoenix?

A. Arizona Mining and Mineral Museum.

—ψ—

Q. To what geological period does the earliest dinosaur ever discovered in the Petrified Forest belong?

A. The Triassic Period, more than 200 million years ago.

Q. What state park near Cottonwood features both desert highland and wetland habitats and wildlife?

A. Dead Horse Ranch State Park.

—ψ—

Q. It is estimated that the volcano at Sunset Crater last erupted how long ago?

A. Around nine hundred years.

—ψ—

Q. The clustered pincushion is a species of cacti whose range is limited to Arizona, especially which Indian reservation?

A. Tohono O'odham.

—ψ—

Q. How many species of hummingbird have been spotted at Ramsey Canyon Preserve near Sierra Vista?

A. Fourteen.

—ψ—

Q. Who operates Ramsey Canyon Preserve?

A. The Nature Conservancy.

—ψ—

Q. Where did Dr. C. Hart Merriam develop his concept of "life zones" as one travels from low to high ground?

A. On Arizona's San Francisco Peak.

—ψ—

Q. Arizona's higher, cooler mountain and plateau country promotes growth of what kind of tree, to produce the largest forest of its kind in the United States?

A. Ponderosa pine.

Q. Who wrote the book *Arizona and Its Bird Life*?

A. Herbert Brandt.

—ψ—

Q. Some Native Americans in the Southwest used the yucca plant for what two purposes?

A. Shampoo/soap and cord.

—ψ—

Q. What poisonous lizard lives in Arizona and other parts of the Southwest?

A. Gila monster.

—ψ—

Q. Completed in 1991, what is the Central Arizona Project?

A. A 336-mile system of canals, tunnels, and pipelines from Lake Havasu on the Colorado River to St. Xavier Indian Reservation, designed to ensure the state a sufficient supply of water.

—ψ—

Q. What zoo is in Tucson?

A. Reid Park.

—ψ—

Q. Cochise County is an especially attractive place for what variety of cacti to grow?

A. Golf ball pincushion.

—ψ—

Q. What writer and naturalist wrote *The Desert Year*?

A. Joseph Wood Krutch.

Q. What activist wrote prolifically about environmental subjects?

A. Edward Abbey.

Q. Edward Abbey wrote what widely read book about the southwestern desert?

A. *Desert Solitaire.*

Q. What is mescal, as in the name Mescal Mountains?

A. A spineless cactus from which the drug peyote is derived.

Q. What three rare members of the cat family inhabit only the extreme southeastern part of Arizona and parts of New Mexico, Texas, and Mexico?

A. Jaguar, ocelot, and jaguarundi cat.

Q. What wealthy Bostonian used his own money to build the Lowell Observatory?

A. Percival Lowell.

Q. In what year was the Desert Botanical Garden opened for the public in Phoenix?

A. 1939.

Q. Devoted exclusively to arid land plants of the world, the Desert Botanical Garden contains how many acres?

A. Approximately150 acres.

Q. The four recreational areas of Echo Canyon, North Mountain Recreation Area, South Mountain Park, and Squaw Peak Park are contained within what preserve?

A. Phoenix Mountains Preserve.

—ψ—

Q. What is the largest city park in the world?

A. South Mountain Park, Phoenix, containing 16,500 acres.

—ψ—

Q. How many acres does the entire Phoenix Mountains Preserve contain?

A. 23,500.

—ψ—

Q. What is the state flower of Arizona?

A. The saguaro cactus blossom.

—ψ—

Q. Where is Camelback Mountain located?

A. Within Echo Canyon.

—ψ—

Q. What park in Phoenix contains a zoo, hiking paths, facilities for horseback riding, and a natural wonder called "Hole in the Rock"?

A. Papago Park.

—ψ—

Q. What Phoenix museum houses more than 350 hands-on exhibits?

A. The Arizona Science Center.

Q. In figuring water supply, one acre-foot (one acre of water one foot deep) will supply approximately how many city dwellers for one year?

A. Five.

Q. Which species of cacti is sometimes called "Queen of the Night"?

A. Night-blooming cereus.

Q. What did the Native Americans make from the tuber of night-blooming cereus?

A. An intoxicating liquid called *tulapai*.

Q. What is the largest dry cavern in the world?

A. Colossal Cave.

Q. Where is Colossal Cave located?

A. Twenty miles east of Tucson.

Q. In 1980 what Arizona State University astronomer discovered evidence that the quasar identified as 3C273 may constitute the center of a galaxy?

A. Susan Wyckoff.

Q. Because of the limited amount of water available for irrigation, about what portion of Arizona's soil is suitable for farming?

A. One eighth.

Q. Who designed the Arizona Science Center?

A. Antoine Predock.

—ψ—

Q. How many different bird species have been spotted in the Madera Canyon Recreational area south of Tucson?

A. Four hundred.

—ψ—

Q. What is Arizona's southeasternmost national wildlife refuge?

A. San Bernardino.

—ψ—

Q. Seven pollination gardens showing interaction among insects, birds, bats, and plants is one feature of what Tucson museum?

A. Arizona-Sonora Desert Museum.

—ψ—

Q. The world-famous Mayo Clinic has a branch in what Arizona city?

A. Scottsdale.

—ψ—

Q. What is Arizona's number-one agricultural product?

A. Cotton.

—ψ—

Q. After cotton, what are the three chief crops—all foods— grown in Arizona?

A. Lettuce, cauliflower, and broccoli.

Q. Where is the annual Southwest Wings Birding Festival held?

A. Sierra Vista.

—ψ—

Q. When was the telescope at Kitt Peak placed into operation?

A. 1964.

—ψ—

Q. What is the size of the reflecting telescope at Kitt Peak?

A. 213 centimeters, or 84 inches.

—ψ—

Q. What is the state gem?

A. Turquoise.

—ψ—

Q. Which variety of cholla cacti is common in southern Arizona at altitudes up to three thousand feet?

A. The jumping cholla.

—ψ—

Q. How tall can a jumping cholla grow?

A. Up to about fifteen feet.

—ψ—

Q. How many acres does the Phoenix Zoo contain?

A. 125.

—ψ—

Q. In what county is Organ Pipe National Monument located?

A. Pima.

Q. From what park near downtown Phoenix can one view the city?

A. Squaw Peak Park.

—ψ—

Q. The Joshua tree is a member of what large plant family?

A. It is a species of yucca within the lily family.

—ψ—

Q. Sometimes called Spanish bayonet, yucca also goes by what name?

A. Our Lord's candle.

—ψ—

Q. In what location is the broadleaf yucca primarily found?

A. Desert country of southern Arizona.

—ψ—

Q. In 1977 what did University of Arizona astronomers discover?

A. Information supporting the nebula hypothesis of planet formation.

—ψ—

Q. What Apache tribe takes its name from the mescal plant?

A. Mescalero Apaches.

—ψ—

Q. The Boyce Thompson Arboretum, a thirty-five-acre living museum, is located near what town?

A. Superior.

Q. What institution administers the Boyce Thompson Arboretum?

A. University of Arizona.

—ψ—

Q. The twin volcanoes near Eagar that last erupted nearly seven hundred thousand years ago go by what name?

A. The Twin Knolls.

—ψ—

Q. The Apache-Sitgreaves National Forest contains how many acres?

A. Approximately two million.

—ψ—

Q. What museum in Scottsdale honors a large mammal?

A. Buffalo Museum of America.

—ψ—

Q. The Pinaleno Mountains in Graham County are known for what variety of cacti?

A. Leding's hedgehog.

—ψ—

Q. By 1890 the production of what metal had exceeded gold and silver in value in Arizona?

A. Copper.

—ψ—

Q. In what year was the observatory at Northern Arizona University opened?

A. 1952.

Q. What Arizona mammal dines on prickly pear cacti, spines and all?

A. Javelina.

—ψ—

Q. What is the size of Northern Arizona University's telescope?

A. Twenty-four inches.

—ψ—

Q. What rare American bird has been spotted from time to time at the Ramsey Canyon Preserve?

A. Golden eagle.

—ψ—

Q. When did a speeding meteor create Meteor Crater?

A. About fifty thousand years ago.

—ψ—

Q. What are the dimensions of Meteor Crater?

A. Approximately one mile across, three miles in circumference, and six hundred feet deep.

—ψ—

Q. To what age can the saguaro cactus grow?

A. As much as two hundred years old.

—ψ—

Q. What geologist, authority on irrigation, student of Native Americans, and explorer became director of the Bureau of American Ethnology in 1879 and of the U.S. Geological Survey in 1881?

A. John Wesley Powell.

Q. When was Arizona's first copper mine opened for operation?

A. 1854 at Ajo.

—ψ—

Q. For what reason was the Cabeza Prieta National Wildlife Refuge originally created?

A. To protect bighorn sheep and other endangered desert wildlife.

—ψ—

Q. What national monument in the state is named for a particular type of uncommon cactus?

A. Organ Pipe Cactus National Monument.

—ψ—

Q. What Tucson institution serves as headquarters for Native Seeds/SEARCH, an organization that studies and markets native plants and their seeds?

A. The Tucson Botanical Gardens.

—ψ—

Q. What four counties have the most productive irrigated areas in the state?

A. La Paz, Maricopa, Pinal, and Yuma.

—ψ—

Q. Part of what national forest touches Tucson on the northeast?

A. Coronado.

—ψ—

Q. One of the world's largest collections of fire-fighting equipment, dating from 1725, is found in what museum?

A. Hall of Flame Museum of Firefighting in Phoenix.

Q. The Sedona-Oak Creek Canyon area is in the heart of what colorful territory?

A. Red Rock.

—ψ—

Q. What is the state fossil?

A. Petrified wood.

—ψ—

Q. Pluto's only moon, Charon, was discovered by astronomers in 1978 at an observatory in what city?

A. Flagstaff.

—ψ—

Q. Where would you go to visit the Arizona Mining and Mineral Museum?

A. Phoenix.

—ψ—

Q. What prehistoric people in Arizona were the first in the New World to irrigate their agricultural crops?

A. The Hohokam.

—ψ—

Q. Which Arizona national park is divided into two parts, with one section lying east of Tucson and the other one lying west?

A. Saguaro.

—ψ—

Q. Who was the first person to suggest damming the Colorado River for water storage purposes?

A. Dr. Elwood Mead, after whom Lake Mead was named, in 1897.

Q. Which part of Saguaro National Park, the east or the west, is the larger?

A. The east, with 67,000 acres; the west section contains about 24,000.

—ψ—

Q. What organization provided the nation's first nongovernmental, nonprofit, nonsectarian, Native American–operated health care system?

A. The Navajo Health Foundation at Ganado.

—ψ—

Q. When it was completed in 1936, what record did Hoover (Boulder) Dam hold?

A. World's largest dam.

—ψ—

Q. Often incorrectly thought to be a variety of cacti, what Arizona plant is also called coachwhip?

A. Ocotillo.

—ψ—

Q. Because the terrain is similar to that of the moon, NASA once trained astronauts at what Arizona site?

A. Meteor Crater, near Winslow.

—ψ—

Q. What 1870 cattle ranch, now preserved as a national monument, received the first telegraph in Arizona?

A. Pipe Spring.

—ψ—

Q. What is unique about Saguaro National Park?

A. It contains the world's largest growth of the giant saguaro cacti.

Q. How did the Bright Angel Trail in the Grand Canyon come into being?

A. Originally a wild animal path, it was adopted by the Havasupai Indians.

—ψ—

Q. Each January and February the population of the small town of Quartzsite swells to one million people for what reason?

A. To visit the gem and mineral shows in the area.

—ψ—

Q. What do Arizonans call Groundhog Day?

A. Agua Fria Freddie Day.

—ψ—

Q. What Tucson museum houses more than twenty-two thousand mineral samples?

A. The University of Arizona Mineralogical Museum.

—ψ—

Q. What park salutes five centuries of transportation across the Colorado River?

A. Yuma Crossing State Historic Park.

—ψ—

Q. Of what observatory in Tucson was Andrew Elliott Douglass once director?

A. Steward Observatory.

—ψ—

Q. If a building is situated on the Colorado River "meander," where is it?

A. Where the river bends.

Q. More than two hundred aircraft, including the Air Force One plane that was used by Presidents Kennedy and Johnson, are housed at what museum near Tucson?

A. Pima Air and Space Museum.

—ψ—

Q. What is the origin of the word *cactus*, a plant very common in Arizona?

A. It is from the Greek *kaktos*, meaning "prickly plant."

—ψ—

Q. What are the record high and low temperatures for Phoenix?

A. 122 degrees and 16 degrees.

—ψ—

Q. What two visually dominant life forms separate the Sonoran Desert from other North American deserts?

A. Legume trees and columnar cacti.

—ψ—

Q. With what metal is the dome of the Arizona State Capitol covered?

A. Copper.

—ψ—

Q. What was the first skyscraper to be built in Arizona?

A. Heard Building, Phoenix.

—ψ—

Q. Near what town is a field where meteorites that exploded and fragmented at high altitudes are dispersed in a zone covering a couple of square miles?

A. Holbrook.

Q. Within Pima County's Tucson Mountain Park, what environmental and scientific educational institution founded in 1986 conducts research on native arthropods, flowering plants, and meteorology?

A. Sonoran Arthropod Studies Institute.

Q. What are arthropods?

A. Any animal belonging to the major division called *Arthropoda*, which includes insects, like beetles and butterflies; crustaceans, like crabs and lobsters; arachnids, like spiders and scorpions; centipedes; and millipedes.

Q. How much concrete was used in the construction of Hoover Dam?

A. 3.25 million cubic feet.

Q. Poisonous to livestock, what Arizona plant is useful as a soap substitute?

A. Amole, a species of the agave plant.

Q. Smoke from the wood of what Arizona plant is ideal for barbecues?

A. Mesquite.

Q. In what county is coal obtained from surface mines?

A. Navajo.

Q. After World War II use of what technology contributed greatly to Arizona's population increase?

A. Air conditioning.

Q. In 1963 why did the U.S. Supreme Court give Arizona rights to water from the Colorado River?

A. The state was pumping more water from its underground water supply than it was getting from rainfall.

—ψ—

Q. U. S. Supreme Court allotted Arizona how many acre-feet of water each year from the Colorado River?

A. 2.8 million.

—ψ—

Q. In 1984 what University of Arizona astronomer photographed a planetary system in formation?

A. Bradford A. Smith.

—ψ—

Q. What are the chief fishing catches in Lake Mead?

A. Largemouth bass, striped bass, and catfish.

—ψ—

Q. What percentage of native North American wildlife lives within Arizona's boundaries?

A. 60 percent.

—ψ—

Q. When is it estimated that the last volcanic eruption occurred in Arizona?

A. In about A.D. 1064.

—ψ—

Q. Where is the Navajo Nation Zoological and Botanical Park located?

A. Window Rock.

Q. What two commodities are the primary elements of adobe?

A. Mud and straw.

Q. What monthly Internet-based magazine has as its purpose to entertain, educate, and explore the beauty, life, and culture of North American deserts?

A. *DesertUSA.*

Q. Near what town can million-year-old fossilized dinosaur tracks be viewed?

A. Tuba City.

Q. What endangered species of bird was recently introduced into the Grand Canyon?

A. California condor.

Q. How have greatly diminished populations of coyote and other predators caused irreparable damage to cacti in Arizona?

A. Lack of predators has produced too many desert rodents that feed on and nest in cacti.

Q. What wildlife haven, famous for its tens of thousands of migrating birds, was preserved when Imperial Dam was built?

A. Imperial National Wildlife Refuge.

Q. Where is the building used in the Biosphere project, in which eight people lived for two years under a glass dome?

A. Tucson.

Q. From what native plant is the liquor tequila made?

A. Agave.

–ψ–

Q. Since removing any petrified wood of any size from the Petrified Forest is punishable by heavy fines and imprisonment, where do the polished specimens come from that are sold in nearby curio shops?

A. Privately owned land outside the park.

–ψ–

Q. Along I-10 and I-8, alert signs with changeable messages are posted to warn motorists of what natural hazards?

A. Dust storms.

–ψ–

Q. When during the day is the Painted Desert particularly beautiful?

A. Sunrise and sunset, when the colors are most brilliant and the shadows the deepest.

–ψ–

Q. Some of the world's oldest and largest Fremont cottonwood trees are found in what preserve?

A. Patagonia-Sonoita Creek.

–ψ–

Q. How was London Birdge transported to Arizona?

A. Block by block, reassembled in its original form.

–ψ–

Q. For seekers of fire agates and other semiprecious stones, two rockhound areas near Safford are maintained by what agency?

A. U.S. Bureau of Land Management.

Q. How high is Tonto Natural Bridge, among the world's largest such formations?

A. 183 feet, with the opening beneath 150 feet wide and 400 feet long.

—ψ—

Q. The area around what town draws visitors because it is believed to contain several vortexes of electromagnetic energy rising up from the earth to energize and inspire people?

A. Sedona.

—ψ—

Q. Of the fifty-four Titan Intercontinental Ballistic Missiles (ICBMs) in the United States, all have been destroyed except one, which is located at what tourist attraction?

A. Titan Missile Museum in Green Valley.

—ψ—

Q. In February and August the people of what town gather to bid goodbye to the Desert Caballeros who then ride into the Bradshaw Mountains to camp out?

A. Wickenburg.

—ψ—

Q. The site of the U.S. Army Electronic Proving Ground, what fort is headquarters for the army Information Systems Command and other operations?

A. Fort Huachuca.

—ψ—

Q. A broad, flat-topped elevation with one or more cliff-like sides common in the Southwest is called a mesa, which means what in Spanish?

A. "Tabletop."

Q. The one hundred-square-mile Sonoran Desert that covers most of the southern half of Arizona, extends into what four other geographical entities?

A. Southeastern California, most of the Baja California peninsula, the islands in the Gulf of California, and much of the Mexican state of Sonora.

Q. In 1883 what group founding Mesa discovered the canal system used by the ancient inhabitants and used it to irrigate their farmland?

A. Mormons.

Q. Before they discovered true writing, the early Native Americans used what two kinds of symbols to communicate with each other and to record history?

A. Petroglyphs and pictographs.

Q. What is the difference between petroglyphs and pictographs?

A. A petroglyph is scratched or carved onto a rock with another rock, and a pictograph is painted on the surface of the rock.

Q. Western International University, a private educational institution with flexible scheduling at night and on weekends, focused on global and technological issues, is beginning what new program?

A. Certified Financial Planner to prepare students for the certification exam to obtain a license.